V C

P9-CEM-038

Please remember that this is a library book,
and that it belongs only temporarily to each
person who uses it. Be considerate. Do
not write in this, or any, library book.

# BUDDHISM

## A Way
### of Life
### and Thought

WITHDRAWN

# BUDDHISM

## A Way
## of Life
## and Thought

Nancy Wilson Ross

WITHDRAWN

Vintage Books

A Division of Random House   New York

First Vintage Books Edition, October 1981
Copyright © 1980 by Nancy Wilson Ross
All rights reserved under International and Pan-American
Copyright Conventions. Published in the United States by
Random House, Inc., New York, and simultaneously in Canada
by Random House of Canada Limited, Toronto. Originally
published by Alfred A. Knopf, Inc., New York, in November 1980.
Owing to limitations of space, all acknowledgments of
permission to reprint previously published material, and to
reproduce illustrations, will be found following the index.

Library of Congress Cataloging in Publication Data
Ross, Nancy Wilson, 1905-
Buddhism, a way of life and thought.
Bibliography: p.
Includes index.
1. Buddhism.   I. Title.
[BQ4022.R67   1981]   294.3   81-40081
ISBN 0-394-74754-2   AACR2

Manufactured in the United States of America
B 876

This book is gratefully and affectionately dedicated
to Richard Dudley Baker, the Roshi and Abbot
of the San Francisco Zen Center, through whose generosity
I was provided with personal assistants during the long, slow process
of completing this work
against heavy odds of health and circumstance.

I have often been asked how I, coming from a long line of Christians of different denominations, including, in various family branches, Presbyterians, Congregationalists, Unitarians and Episcopalians, happened in midlife to turn to the alien faith of Buddhism. It would not be easy to give a short answer to this question, and I was therefore happy to come on some lines from Antoine de Saint-Exupéry which seemed to me to express my feelings.

. . . Of what can we be certain except this—that we are fertilized by mysterious circumstances? Where is man's truth to be found? Truth is not that which can be demonstrated by the air of logic. If orange-trees are hardy and rich in fruit in this bit of soil and not that, then this bit of soil is what is truth for orange-trees. If a particular religion, or culture, or scale of values, if one form of activity rather than another, brings self-fulfillment to a man, releases the prince within him unknown to himself, then that scale of values, that culture, that form of activity constitute his truth.

—Antoine de Saint-Exupéry
(*Wind, Sand, and Stars*)

# Contents

# Acknowledgments

Special mention and my warmest thanks go to John Bailes for his two years of patient, efficient and cheerful assistance in research, in typing and retyping, in reading and re-reading (often aloud); and also for similar services, although for a lesser stretch of time, to Lynn Hesselbart.

Lama Anagarika Govinda, Richard Baker-roshi, Lionel Landry, executive director of the Asia Society, Dr. Kathleen Raine, and Blythe Morley Brennan have my enduring gratitude for their conscientious reading of the manuscript at a critical time and for offering valuable suggestions.

Toinette Lippe at Knopf has remained, throughout, a devoted and effective editor.

Finally and personally, I cannot omit a list of names of young people whose presence in my household at different times in the last few years gave me encouragement and a variety of supports when and where they were most needed. In chronological order, they are: Yvonne Rand, Renée des Tombe, Richard Levine, Lucy McClintock, Karin Gjording, Deborah Madison, Dan Welch and Linda Cutts. Without them this book would never have been finished.

N. W. R.

# The Buddha's Life Story and Basic Teachings

Buddhism, the religion of reason and meditation, was born in India in the sixth century before Christ and, down succeeding centuries, spread over vast stretches of Asia. Today it is estimated that between one-third and one-fifth of the people on earth follow some aspect of this many-aspected religious philosophy, and their number is steadily increasing, not only in Asian countries like India—where Buddhism originated, declined and is now reviving—but also in modern Europe and America. Many modern Westerners now study and practice Zen; others have formed communities under the guidance of exiled Tibetans or have taken instruction in Theravada Buddhism with teachers from Burma, Sri Lanka or Thailand.

In a gentle way, without militant crusades or unyielding dogmatic emphases—with, on the contrary, the quiet force of what might be considered historic inevitability—Buddhism from its beginning slowly spread out from northeastern India. Moving southward and westward during and immediately after the founder's time and, later, far to the east by way of the legendary silk routes and maritime passages from the southeastern coasts of the Indian subcontinent and the adjacent converted islands, it became in time the dominant influence in vast sections of Asia. Burma, Sri Lanka,

Thailand, Cambodia, Vietnam, Laos, Mongolia, Tibet, Nepal, Bhutan, Sikkim, China, Korea and Japan are all countries which have been affected significantly by Buddhism. In the United States, Buddhist teaching centers are now scattered across the country from New England to California, and it is worth noting that in Hawaii, America's newest state, Buddhism is the major religious denomination.

During its long centuries of quiet pilgrimage by land and sea, much of Buddhism's powerful influence may have had its source in the deliberate avoidance of claims to exclusive Truth, adherence to inflexible dogma, or the authority of any final, sacrosanct, theocratic hierarchy. The "Come and see for yourself" attitude of the original Great Teacher, Siddhartha Gautama, who became the Buddha, the Enlightened One, his pragmatic insistence on "Don't take my word for it. Try it yourself!" the unswerving challenge of his famous aphorism, "Look within, *thou* art the Buddha"—all this served to lower the resistance that so often attends the arrival of a new and unfamiliar faith. There can be no doubt that Buddhism contained, and still contains, the power to evoke original responses from many different cultures. It has stimulated people of different ethnic backgrounds to quickened creativity, to new syntheses and syncretisms which, oftener than not, have transcended narrow regionalism. The many subtle cross-fertilizations which Buddhism helped foster in the past are most easily traceable in works of art, but they are also exemplified in much of the literature of different sections of Asia, notably of Tibet, China and Japan.

What, then, was the origin of this exceptional religious philosophy which, in spite of its followers' cultural differences, so plainly reflected in diverse forms of art, in varying attitudes toward ways of worship, and even in methods for attaining the final Buddhist goal, Enlightenment, could retain for more than 2,500 years a basic continuity and homogeneity?

Buddhism, unlike Hinduism—that other great India-born religion, which has not flourished notably outside the geographic boundaries of the Indian subcontinent—is not a "revealed" religion. It was founded by a specific human being, the so-called historic

Buddha, born Siddhartha Gautama in northwestern India six centuries before the Christian era. Any account of Buddhism must, therefore, properly begin with the oft-told story of the life of this remarkable religious genius.

The Buddha was the son of an aristocrat; "rajah" is the title most often given his father, although in some accounts he is called a "king." The designation "rajah" serves well enough to indicate the kind of circumstances into which Siddhartha, a long-awaited heir, was born. He was born in a small Indian kingdom located on the southern borders of the Himalayan country known today as Nepal, roughly 100 miles north and east of the modern Indian city of Benares. His family belonged to one of the two leading castes of India, the Kshatriya, the aristocratic military class, equal in social standing to the priestly Brahmins but less involved in sacerdotal affairs.

The circumstances of the Buddha's birth and early life lent a specific force to his later teachings. When he declared that no distinctions of caste or former occupation should stand in the way of anyone who wished to become a disciple, he was speaking from a position of hereditary privilege that he had voluntarily relinquished. Upon occasion he emphasized his belief that Brahmins, those all-powerful guides and spiritual authorities who dominated Indian society, were no better than anyone else just by reason of their exalted birth. Only if they comported themselves in a manner worthy of honor had they the right to claim the privileges of superior status. This declaration fell little short of what Western religious terminology would label as heresy, since at that time the Brahmins were the indisputable spiritual arbiters of Indian life.

At his birth and during his youth Siddhartha Gautama had, one might say, "everything." Like so many of today's searching, dissatisfied young people, he grew up in a world of affluence and privilege. His father, Suddhodana, centered his own life around that of his son and heir. Legends relate that not only did he anticipate and grant every whim or fancy that might cross the mind of an indulged child, he even took the strictest precautions to prevent Siddhartha's experiencing any distressing incidents that could cast the slightest shadow on his happiness. To this end the rajah went so far as to forbid his son, even after he reached manhood, to go outside the protective boundaries of the palace compound.

Siddhartha, restless and curious, chose not to obey these parental rules and, so the story goes, during several secret and forbidden ventures outside the palace grounds he encountered four unsettling sights which are known in Buddhist lore as the Four Signs. The first of these Signs was an old man. The second a very sick man. The third a corpse. Until then the protected prince had never fully realized what decrepit old age could mean in the way of weakness and disability. He had no true sense of the toll taken of the physical body by serious illness, nor had he imagined the effect that the utter finality of death could have on the bereaved mourners remaining behind. Deeply disturbed by his growing awareness of life's tragic side, he had no one to talk to or question but Channa, the companion and charioteer who had regularly accompanied him on his secret forays outside the palace gates. To all of his questions Channa could only reply with infinite sadness, "Yes, master, there is no escape. Old age, sickness, death—such is the lot of all men."

In increasing anxiety, Siddhartha began to ask himself how it is possible for anyone truly to enjoy living, feel happy, experience lasting pleasure, when finally, for everyone, without exception, there is no escape from suffering, sadness, loss and, at the end, inevitable personal extinction. Why should a man wish to be born at all; for that matter, why should anyone even wish to *give* birth?

He could find no one within the palace circle to answer his disquieting questions and troubled musings. One day, however, when again wandering outside the palace gates, he chanced to see a passing ascetic with calm eyes and a face expressing both purpose and detachment. This was the fourth of the Four Signs. It pointed him in a new direction and gave him what he needed to know; Like this wandering holy man with his alms bowl and simple garments, he too must leave the place of his birth and go forth into a homeless wayfaring life. He would begin by seeking out the wisest sages, no matter how distant, in the hope that they could tell him how to meet life's sufferings and difficulties, and, even more important, what life's meaning really was.

Although the fourth of the Four Signs, the wandering mendicant, had convinced Siddhartha that he could no longer remain in the palace compound, he had, by now, a beautiful wife and a son, and they created ties far more difficult to break than all the luxuries he had for so long accepted without thought. Yet there was for him no choice. He knew without question that he must soon leave forever the gracious life into which he had been born. And so there came a night when, without daring even to touch his little son for fear the child might awaken his wife, who would plead with him not to go (or even, perhaps, arouse the guards to prevent his departure), he took a long tender look at them both as they slept and, for the last time, stole outside the palace gates with his devoted companion Channa. He was in his twenties and more than fifty years of search and teaching lay ahead.

The Great Departure, as it is known in Buddhist lore, this silent and secret leave-taking of a young wife and first-born son, appears on the surface to indicate a heartlessness similar to that of the Christian Savior who in Luke 14:26 stated, "If any man come to me and hate not his father and mother and wife and children and brethren and sisters . . . he cannot be my disciple"—a passage that does not readily lend itself to easy or comforting interpretation.

The adoption of a wandering religious life, in particular among the upper classes, has never been uncommon in India. To this day it is a familiar and accepted feature of Indian society. Any man or woman, after fulfilling his or her duties as a householder and head of a family, has the right, if so desired, to live in solitude, given over wholly to the religious quest, which is not seen as an accompaniment to conventional worldly activities but as an actual and honorable *occupation in itself.*

Siddhartha was a little young to set forth on this rigorous solitary course. Such drastic withdrawals usually come to Indians after middle life. But, as we shall see, Buddha's eventual tenets of teaching and practice ran somewhat counter to the prevailing religious modes of his era, even though he continued to make use of a number of ancient spiritual concepts and a vocabulary which contained such commonly used metaphysical terms as *karma* and *nirvana*— the first of which, one's inherited "fate," had to be conquered in order to reach the latter, total "release."

Of the Buddha's final departure from home Buddhist artists have carved and painted many delightful imaginary scenes like the one in which attendant aerial deities hold aloft the hooves of the prince's horse so they will make no sound as the young man leaves home forever on the first steps of his long wayfaring. In this representation of the Great Departure it is notable that the prince himself does not appear; the horse is riderless. This illustrates an early and relatively short-lived view that after his supreme enlightenment the Buddha could not properly be represented in human form. While this iconographic convention was being observed, we find, therefore, in scenes from his later career, his presence indicated only by such symbols as an unoccupied throne, footprints, an open umbrella, a wheel.

Now, however, in his life story the Buddha-to-be is just putting behind him his princely existence. Some legends recount how he exchanged his costly garments with a passing woodcutter; some describe how he cut off his dark locks, worn long and flowing as befitted an aristocrat, to send back to his family as a memento. Other stories of this hair-cutting relate that when he used his sword on his hair, it was reduced to "two fingers in length" and, curling itself to the right around his head, remained there, in this fashion, for the rest of his days. This curled topknot of hair is seen on the earliest representations of the Buddha image made in the ancient northwestern kingdom of Gandhara, now in Pakistan and Afghanistan. Alexander the Great had invaded Gandhara in 327 B.C., and as a consequence its early Buddhist art, created by transplanted Mediterranean artists, reflects certain stylistic influences from the distant Greco-Roman world. To the indigenous Indian artist the Buddha's topknot, or *ushnisha*, was more than merely a style of hairdressing; it represented a part of a "divine anatomy," an actual extrusion of the skull indicating the presence of cosmic consciousness or a highly developed intuitive intelligence. This was not a symbol with which transplanted Greco-Roman artists could identify, just as they did not possess any prototype for a figure seated in formal meditation posture. Their solution to the Buddha's *ushnisha* was the curled topknot of hair associated with representations of their own god Apollo and, as Benjamin Rowland has told us, a Buddha figure's folded legs, locked in the—to them— unfamiliar *padmasana*, were artfully concealed under voluminous draperies.

To return to the story of the Great Departure, another of the several legends that grew up around it relates significantly to the role of nature and animals in Buddhist lore. Gautama's faithful horse, Kanthaka, who had come into existence at the time of the future Buddha's birth, died of a broken heart on parting with his master and was immediately "reborn as a god." This legendary detail is suggestive of Buddhism's belief in the possible progression of all living forms from lower to higher levels, a theme extensively set forth in the *Jatakas*, or Life Stories of the Buddha. A collection of rather Aesop-like tales which trace the Buddha's former animal and human incarnations, the *Jatakas* might be said to be, in effect, a very early allegorical expression of the theory of evolution.*

In India from the earliest times there were many sages, or gurus, who lived apart from ordinary existence in quiet forests or lonely caves and were willing to share their spiritual explorations and conclusions with other earnest seekers. The future Buddha therefore did not have far to go in his search for a spiritual guide. One of the most notable of contemporary pundits, a recluse named Alara Kalama, undertook to answer the young man's troubled questions, to supply him with learned replies and to suggest means of discipline designed to quiet his troubled mind.

In spite, however, of Alara Kalama's profound wisdom and personal interest, Siddhartha failed to find any deep inner satisfaction in what he was being taught. He therefore, after a time, left Alara Kalama and went to another famous sage of the period named Uddaka. Here again he discovered that, although he learned a great deal about philosophical matters and methods of bodily discipline, this knowledge still did not serve to answer his most profound questions.

Again he departed from his teacher and after a period of

---

* See Bishop P. Bigandet, *Life and Legend of the Buddha*, London, Kegan Paul, Trench, Trubner & Co. Ltd., 1914; N. W. Ross, *Three Ways of Asian Wisdom*, New York, Simon and Schuster, 1966.

wandering he came to the town of Uruvela, where, on the outskirts, finding a pleasant grove of trees with flowing water nearby, he sat down in the company of five fellow seekers to undertake an indefinite period of unbroken meditation and strict asceticism.

For six years he remained in this place, practicing the most extreme austerities while attempting to keep his mind firmly fixed on the intention of his original quest. During this time he conquered many physical appetites and disabilities and learned how, in the yogic way, to hold "the mad monkey of the mind" unremittingly steady. And yet he still did not feel that he had found any real "release," or answers to the questions posed him by the Three Signs: old age, sickness and death. What was more, in practicing excessive physical deprivation, he had so wasted his body that it could barely sustain the force of his continuous driving search.

In Buddhist art there are sculptured images of this period in the Buddha's life which show a man who has deliberately starved himself, deprived his body of many of its most insistent and distracting needs until every bone and sinew can be seen beneath the tightly stretched skin, and the skull is a virtual death's head.

It was at this point, on the very brink of death from self-imposed denial of the body's physical needs, that Siddhartha had the illumination which so effectively indicates a break with many of the practices of ancient Hindu yoga—in particular with certain extreme types of hatha yoga which teach that only by total and, in the Western view, fanatic conquering of the physical body can another and higher stage of consciousness be reached.

What the future Buddha realized was that he, a human creature, had only one instrument through which to attain his goal. This instrument was the physical body in which his brain, his heart, and his entire human consciousness were housed. Why then was he abusing this once perfect instrument, sternly denying its fundamental needs?

*The "Starving Buddha" during his period of extreme asceticism, before he realized that his body, as the one instrument of possible enlightenment, should therefore not be abused. Gandhara. Second–third century A.D.*

As soon as he recognized the extremism and futility of the course he had been pursuing, Siddhartha decided to take nourishing food again and attempt to live a more normal existence while still continuing the determined pursuit of his goal. Thereupon, to the disgust of the companions who had marveled at his staunch self-denial for so many years, Siddhartha rose, went forth and once again begged food in the nearby village.

When they observed this seemingly irresolute behavior, his five fellow ascetics agreed among themselves that in spite of six years of the most laudable austerities, Siddhartha had plainly retrogressed. Was it likely, they asked themselves, that he would ever achieve enlightenment now that he had gone forth into the villages and partaken once more of the same food as ordinary people who were not involved in such high endeavor? In their disappointment and chagrin, they decided to leave Siddhartha's presence. They took themselves off some distance to a place near Benares, presumably in search of a more reliable source of spiritual inspiration.

The future Buddha, however, restored in mind and body, returned to his meditation under his familiar tree. And shortly thereafter in the Buddha saga we have the events immediately preceding the Great Enlightenment, generally assumed to have taken place in Siddhartha's thirtieth year. At this point a young woman named Sujata, destined to remain eternally celebrated in Buddhist annals, briefly enters the story. Inspired by a night-time vision, she had been moved to prepare a special dish of rice-milk which she presented in a golden bowl to the solitary figure seated under a nearby tree—a figure the girl took to be a divinity because of a special radiance that had begun to shine around him.

The future Buddha graciously accepted Sujata's offering. According to details of one of the several legends, he did not eat again for the forty-nine days that still preceded his Enlightenment. In another version, however, he divided the rice-milk into a number of portions which were to suffice for his nourishment during the

*The Buddha during his pre-Enlightenment meditation, protected by the king of the cobras from storms sent by Mara, the Great Tempter. Siamese. Eleventh–twelfth century. See page 18.*

ensuing days of ever-deepening meditation. Legend also tells how when Siddhartha cast the golden bowl of Sujata's offering into the nearby river it floated *upstream against the current*, coming to rest in the dwelling place of a Serpent King.

These latter details suggest a subtle symbolism. Buddhism, after it became a working faith, was indeed a teaching that had to move upstream *against* the ordinary flow of men's minds. As for the bowl's final resting place in the home of a Serpent King, personifying "Nature's Wisdom," here Buddhism's relation to Nature or the Earth itself seems implied, an implication we find also in a later episode when the Buddha is challenged by Mara, the Tempter, to answer by what "right" he dare call himself enlightened. The Buddha's reply, also a favorite theme in Buddhist art, is given in a

special downward-pointing gesture, or *mudra*, by which he sum-
mons the Earth to give witness to the rightfulness of his claim. He
has fairly earned this supreme designation because of a long series
of unselfish existences through many former incarnations.

After Siddhartha had eaten, thrown the bowl into the river and
watched it move upstream, he ceremoniously bathed and again
returned to his meditation. But this time, when he had seated
himself once more in the lotus posture, he made a fresh vow not
to interrupt himself in any way until he had achieved the state of
supreme awareness toward which he had for so many years been
working. "Though my skin, my nerves and my bones should waste
away and my life-blood dry, I will not leave this seat until I have
attained Supreme Enlightenment."

And the long-sought awakening did come to him while seated
under the fig tree destined in Buddhist history to become the Bodhi
Tree, or Tree of Wisdom, worshipped to this day at a sacred Indian
site, Buddh Gaya. It is here that, in the Buddhist view, "the greatest
event in all human history" took place at the full moon of May in
544 B.C. Supreme Enlightenment had been attained by a man un-
swervingly determined to reach the goal. (Some historians give his
Enlightenment date as fifteen years earlier. The Buddhists of Japan
celebrate a December date. There are other discrepancies in various
legends, which simply indicate that historical accuracy does not
always carry as much weight for the Asian mind as it does for the
Western. Asians on the whole accept the Buddha's awakening as a
great "truth" which had world-shaking consequences. Specific dates
are of minor significance.)

No one, it is said, can possibly explain enlightenment. It does
not lend itself to description or explanation in words. The man who
has awakened, however, is in no doubt about the occurrence. Although unable to describe it, he knows what has happened to him,
just as someone in love may not be able to describe his feelings,
yet is himself in no doubt about his particular physical and emo-

*The Buddha with downstretched right hand (a familiar* mudra), *calling
the earth to witness the legitimacy of his claim to Enlightenment.
Buddhist stele, Burma. Twelfth century.*

tional state, or as a man dying of thirst will know when his thirst is quenched. (As a term, enlightenment signifies a direct, dynamic spiritual experience brought about, in the Buddhist view, through the faculty of intuition, a faculty developed and sharpened by such spiritual disciplines as intensive meditation and contemplation. It is a condition beyond the power and pull of "the opposites," a full realization of the universe and the self *as one*.)

What sets apart the Buddha's Enlightenment from the experiences of other religious figures in world history is the absence of any divine intervention, or transcendent illumination from some

higher-than-human sphere. The truth to which the Buddha came was entirely a discovery made by a human being, brought about by his own efforts. The one way to man's peace, fulfillment and release lay through the calm control of his own mind and senses. Even the original Buddhist goal of nirvana (or "salvation," if one wishes to use a Western term) was the realization that life's meaning lay in the here-and-now and not in some remote realm or celestial state far beyond one's present existence.

At his Enlightenment Gautama saw himself and all life as a vast process, an ever-moving stream of becomings and extinctions, and within this ever-moving flow and interpenetration of energies he recognized as delusion the idea of the existence of an individual ego. What was taken for the "self" was actually a composite of various aggregates, a series of psychophysical reactions and responses with no fixed center or unchanging ego-entity.

This illuminating insight (so modern in its implications) gave Gautama a profound and enduring sense of liberation, delivering him from all ego-drives motivated by greed, hate and delusion. His joy at realizing that he was now free from attachment and desire is given expression in the Dhammapada, an often-translated collection of some four hundred verses setting forth, in general, the Buddha's system of moral philosophy. This song of release, in one of many versions, reads:

> Vainly I sought the builder of my house
> Through countless lives.
> I could not find him. . . .
> How hard it is to tread life after life!
> But now I see you, O builder!
> And never again shall I build my house.
> I have snapped the rafters,
> Split the ridgepole
> And beaten out desire.
> Now my mind is free.*

* *The Dhammapada, The Sayings of the Buddha*, a new rendering by Thomas Byrom, A. A. Knopf, New York, 1976, p. 56.

There are a number of versions of the length of time and the varieties of experience that came to the Buddha immediately following his Enlightenment. Some of the stories tell of his recollection, in the most minute detail, of all the incidents of his many former lives, as well as the construction of the essential points of his future teaching. It was during this period also, according to legend, that Mara, the Tempter, renewed his futile efforts to sway the Buddha from his destiny. But the stones cast at the imperturbable figure by Mara's malign hosts turned to flowers as they fell. The blandishments of Mara's most beautiful daughters proved ineffective. And when Mara, desperate, sent raging storms to force the Buddha from his meditative pose, a Serpent King, Mucalinda, issuing forth from the roots of a nearby tree, wound his body in coils under the serene figure and raised his protective cobra hood until the storms abated.

Mythological serpents in both Buddhism and Hinduism play roles quite unlike that given the Serpent in the Biblical story of the Temptation in the Garden of Eden.* In the Buddhist saga, Mucalinda, the Serpent who represents the Lord of the Earth, by making his body a throne for the Enlightened One and raising his head like an imperial canopy, seems once again to be suggesting not only Buddha's acceptance of the instinctive world of Nature as a part of the *whole* of life but also—yet *without rejection*—an eventual ascendance over the instinctual by way of a higher development of the total self.

It is plain from Buddhism's later teachings that in this enlightened state the Buddha had at last clearly seen the whole universe as a system of interrelated parts, a system composed of various kinds of life of all varieties forever passing from one form to another in a ceaseless flow of energies and appearances.

It can be assumed that an all-wise Teacher would understand in advance the kind of problems which face the propounding of such uncompromising and revolutionary psychological truths as

---

* Recent research indicates, however, that some of the earliest Christian texts, based on Gnostic gospels, did not view the Serpent as evil but as the embodiment of true wisdom. Some texts indeed equate Eve, "the spiritual principle in humanity, with the Snake the Instructor." Elaine Pagels, *The Gnostic Gospels*, New York, Random House, 1979.

those he had come to deliver. How, he asked himself, could he possibly communicate what he knew, a truth "going against the stream, deep, intricate, delicate, hidden, *not to be reached only by mere reasoning*"? Nor by blind faith either, it might be added; for this was a path that demanded unswerving personal effort. By virtue of his achievement of supreme illumination which, in the Buddhist view, severs the bonds of all personal earthly laws and ties, the Buddha could have remained in this state of bliss and detachment and had no further personal contact with human beings; in other words, he had attained nirvana. (For the distinction between *nirvana* and *Parinirvana*—the term for the Buddha's physical death, or Great Demise—see p. 35.)

There was, we are told, a long moment of fearful uncertainty while the very earth "trembled" awaiting the Buddha's decision. In the end, the "Great Buddha Heart of Infinite Compassion prevailed." The Buddha remained among men to teach. (Hinduism was later to lay claim to a part of this cosmic and human triumph: in the Hindu interpretation, it was at the behest of "highest Brahma," the Indian deity who "supervises the process of the unfolding of the flower of the world,"* that the Buddha agreed to reenter the realm of suffering humanity.)

The epochal decision of the Buddha to wander and teach was to become a favorite theme hundreds of years later in the sculptures known as "The Walking Buddha" created by precursors of today's Thais, and in the sensitive art of gifted painters from China and Japan. One of the most famous of the Chinese paintings of this particular moment in the Buddha saga shows a tired, thin, shabby, even sad and anxious man standing on a windy slope, gazing down —with the all-too-human appearance of a person who has had his struggles and must now expect more—into the valley toward which

* *Philosophies of India*, Heinrich Zimmer, New York, Bollingen Series, 1955.

*A Chinese representation—notably humanistic—of the moment in the story of Buddha when he accepts the responsibility of going forth to teach. Liang Kai. Twelfth century.*

he must travel to begin his mission. (This moment in the Buddha's life story is also the theme of Allen Ginsberg's contemporary poem "Sakyamuni Coming Out from the Mountain." See Appendix II.)

Arnold Toynbee, the British historian, has said of the Buddha's decision to go into the world with his teachings that it marks a high point in human development. He sees in this decision a contradiction not only of the Buddha's personal inclination but of his basic doctrines as well. Symbolically it expresses, in Toynbee's view, the personal sacrifice of a sentient being who, although he has found his own release, or salvation, turns back from the "open door" in order to help his fellows attain the state he has reached by unflagging effort through many difficult and weary years—even through many incarnations.

This conduct on the Buddha's part—giving aid to others who are also seeking the path to illumination—was later to become the nexus of the teaching about *Bodhisattvas*, which is an integral part of Buddhist belief in certain Mahayana branches* of Buddhism and has inspired some of Buddhism's greatest works of art. *Bodhisattvas* are enlightened beings on their way to, or arrived at, the state of Buddhahood in which they *voluntarily* postpone their own nirvana while striving to help all forms of sentient life attain "supreme release." *Bodhisattvas* are not to be thought of as Saviors: salvation through another, or "intercessor," was no precept of primitive Buddhism, which, on the contrary, stressed the necessity of achieving the goal of individual enlightenment, becoming an *arhat*, by one's own efforts. The *Bodhisattva*, wise and compassionate, is a being who has passed beyond all "discrimination," has freed himself forever from all ideas of "I," "mine," "yours"; in other words, he no longer has any sense of separateness.

---

* The difference in viewpoint between the two main divisions of Buddhism, the so-called Little Vehicle of Deliverance, or Hinayana (also, and more acceptably, known as the Theravada, or School of the Elders), and the vast Mahayana, or Larger Vehicle, will be taken up in some detail further on.

*The wholly enlightened "Teaching Buddha" in full lotus posture. A supreme example of Gupta art, India (320–600 A.D.). See page 16.*

Here there arises a seeming paradox that might be called the "problem" of the *Bodhisattva*, a problem that appears to involve an insurmountable contradiction. How can one conquer the belief in a separate individuality, with its attendant restrictive sense of "self" and "other," and yet remain acutely aware of both "self" and "other"?

This apparent paradox does not, however, bother Asian philosophers as much as it does their fellows in the West, who, having been bred in the Aristotelian tradition, consider the rational mind man's highest and most valued faculty, even going so far as to

make this "mind" the very center of personal identity.* Buddhist philosophers do not shrink from paradox and contradiction. On the contrary, not only do they seem to accept them easily, as a part of life's inexplicability, they even appear to delight in them. Certainly when Buddhism reaches the development known in China as Ch'an, and in Japan as Zen, the very notion of paradox is a basic platform of the teaching, seen as an inevitable concomitant of the fluid and uncertain human condition.

Not long after the Buddha had made his momentous decision to go forth and attempt to help others set foot on "the path," he encountered his former companions—those who had left him with feelings of disappointment and disgust. They were continuing their usual grim austerities in the Deer Park near Benares (now modern Sarnath, and still a favorite pilgrimage site for Buddhists). As Siddhartha approached through the trees, these once-disapproving ascetics could not help noting that a subtle effulgence seemed to radiate from his very presence. Awe-struck and drawn irresistibly toward him, they went in greeting, prepared to listen to whatever he had come to tell them.

And so, on a summer night of full moon some time in his early thirties, Siddhartha Gautama, now the All-Enlightened Buddha, after first drawing the design of a wheel on the ground in rice grains, preached his initial great sermon, "Setting in Motion the Wheel of the Law (*Dharma*)."

The wheel (*chakra*) is an ancient Indian symbol. Originally probably a sun sign, and later one of the identifying marks of the great Indian god Vishnu, it denotes in yoga a center of physical and psychic energy. When the Buddha drew this wheel on the

* See William Barrett's introduction to D. T. Suzuki's *Zen Buddhism*, New York, Anchor Books, 1956; N. W. Ross, *The World of Zen*, New York, Random House, 1960.

*Mediterranean influences on the earliest Buddhist images (late first century* A.D.*) appear in the art of Gandhara, a section of Northwest India colonized by men from the invading armies of Alexander the Great. See page 8.*

ground he was employing an old, already familiar, Indian symbol to exemplify the eternal karmic round of existence (*samsara*) kept forever in motion by man's unceasing appetite, his thirst (*tanha*), for ego satisfactions of every kind.

What the Buddha had to teach was seemingly, but deceptively, simple. He said, in effect: All humanity is sick. I come therefore to you as a physician who has diagnosed this universal disease and is prepared to help you cure it. The truth of this great sickness can be set forth in four simple statements:

1. No one can deny that suffering (*dukkha*) is a condition of all existence.

2. Suffering and general dissatisfaction come to human beings because they are possessive, greedy and, above all, self-centered.

3. Egocentrism, possessiveness and greed can, however, be understood, overcome, rooted out.

4. This rooting out, this vanquishing, can be brought about by following a simple, reasonable Eightfold Path of be-

havior in thought, word and deed. Change of viewpoint will manifest itself in a new outlook and new patterns of behavior.

What the Buddha was talking about was plainly man's "body-identified mind," as Gerald Heard* once described this universal crippling invalidism. The stages of the Eightfold Path necessary for correcting this tragic state of delusion were set forth by the Buddha as:

1. Right views, or understanding.
2. Right purpose, or aspiration.
3. Right speech.
4. Right conduct.
5. Right livelihood.
6. Right effort.
7. Right kind of awareness or mindfulness.
8. Right concentration, or meditation.

Here we might take note of the fact that the word "right" is not considered by some modern scholars to be an adequate interpretation of the word originally used in this context. "Right," after all, implies a duality which is not characteristic of Buddhist thought. The words "correct" or even "perfect" have been suggested as substitutes. In a book of general nature such as this one, however, the author has felt it best to remain with the now almost universally employed and therefore familiar designation.

Gerald Heard's pragmatic, psychological summation of these eight steps comprising Buddhism's famed Middle Way has a pertinent contemporary ring and might also be given here to help illustrate the Buddha's approach:

1. First you must see clearly what is wrong.
2. Next you must decide that you want to be cured.
3. You must act and
4. speak so as to aim at being cured.

* Anglo-Irish historian and philosopher, 1889–1971.

5. Your livelihood must not conflict with your therapy.
6. That therapy must go forward at the "staying speed," that is, the critical velocity that can be sustained.
7. You must think about it incessantly and
8. learn how to contemplate with the *deep mind.*

These were the basic precepts of the Way of Life which the Buddha undertook to preach in forty-five years of active ministry after he had made the initial great decision to "beat the drum of *Dharma* [truth] in the darkness of the world."

It was not long before the Buddha, by the radiance of his being as well as his fresh vigorous teaching, had many devoted followers, including his former ascetic companions from the forest years. Having announced his intention to proclaim the truth for all humanity, he organized these earliest disciples into bands of monks whom he sent forth on their travels with an exhortation precisely expressive of the purpose behind these endeavors: "Go ye forth, O monks, on your journey, for the profit of the many, for the bliss of the many, out of compassion for the world, for the welfare, for the profit, the bliss of the *devas*\* and mankind. Go not any two together." His concluding remark has a faintly poignant ring: "There will be some who will understand." (A modern Zen Master once advised a group of beginners in a similar vein: "Just sit! Meditate. Someone will join you.")

It should be noted that these wandering followers of the Buddha were not missionaries in the Christian sense of the term. They were not proselytizing for a particular faith, not seeking converts or endeavoring to "save souls." They were simply declaring a self-evident truth "like a mathematician," as one eminent Tibetan has said, "who teaches a scientific fact to those who want to know."

The Buddha taught his followers to repeat a simple three-part formula expressing renunciation of worldly values which is still recited by millions of Buddhists all over the earth:

---

\* *Devas* are a form of nonhuman being, roughly analogous to, and as difficult to explain as, angels. The term is also applied to gods or to mere nature spirits.

I take my refuge in the Buddha.

I take my refuge in the *Dharma*. [*Dhamma* in Pali, i.e., the Teaching.]

I take my refuge in the *Sangha*. [The community of monks. This can also mean the wider community of lay believers.]

This founding of an order of dedicated believers, the *Sangha*, was one of the proofs of the Buddha's psychological acumen, for although he taught that each human being must tread the path to awakening or deliverance alone, he was quite aware of the support to be found in intimate association with others working toward a common goal.

A too-marked separation of the monks of the *Sangha* community from the rest of society was destined in time, however, to contribute to the decline of Buddhism in India. Fanatic invaders—the White Huns and tribes of Islamic faith—came into India from the eighth century on and set about a systematic destruction of indigenous religions. They found the peaceful Buddhists particularly easy targets of aggression because of their distinctive appearance and organized communities for study, work and worship. In time, the greatest Buddhist centers of learning like the University of Nalanda, with reputedly the greatest library of the age, were destroyed; many monks were killed, and many more forced to flee for their lives. Some of those who fled north went to Nepal and Tibet, thereby serving to spread further the Buddha's teaching.

There is a subtle and tragic irony in the fact that Buddhists' shaved heads and yellow robes, along with their special places of residence, could, to bigots of other faiths, signify dangers that warranted violent destruction. In the days of Buddhism's original simplicity, before there were temples and libraries, the dwellings occupied by monks during monsoon seasons, when travel was impossible, were relatively simple shelters. The Buddha himself, never one for outward show, for elaborate rites or conspicuous signs that set the "elect" apart from the laity, had once commented on a monk's traditional garments in humorous mockery, "If the mere wearing of the robe could banish greed, malice and other weaknesses, then as soon as a child was born his friends and kinfolk would make him wear the robe and would press him to wear it, saying, 'Come thou favored of fortune! Come wear the robe; for by the mere wearing of it the greedy will put from them their greed, the malicious their malice and so on.' " He had also characteristically replied when pressed as to the proper dwelling place of practicing Buddhists, "Let those who wish to dwell in the forest, dwell in the forest, and let those who wish to live in the village, live in the village." (Since Buddhism involves a social teaching as well as individual practice, however, it has continued throughout its long history to make use of various conventions in dress and deportment.)

Not only was the Buddha consistent in his lack of interest in matters of monkish dress and abode, he was also disinclined to engage in learned argumentation on such debatable and essentially unsolvable matters as the nature of divinity, first causes, life after death and similar subjects. One of the most apt illustrations of this invariably pragmatic position can be found in his replies to a disciple named Malunkyaputta, who had been striving in vain to engage the Master in learned dialectic of the kind presumably then favored among Indian gurus. In some irritation because of the lack of response on the Teacher's part, this monk, with his restive, overactive, impatient mind, finally remarked that he would either get some answers to his persistent queries or leave the Order.

To this ultimatum the Buddha replied in effect that such an attitude could only be compared to that of a man who, having been shot with a poisoned arrow, says, "I will not remove this arrow, call a physician, or heal my wound until I have ascertained who shot the arrow, what tribe he belonged to, how the arrow was made and so on." Or, perhaps, to a man in a burning house who declares, "I will not leave the house until I find out who set the fire in the first place."

In the Buddha's view, intellectual exchanges, which can never be more than theoretical, were mere pedagogy, a waste of vital energy. "Whether the doctrine obtains, Malunkyaputta, that the world is eternal or that the world is not eternal, there still remain birth, old age and death, sorrow, lamentations, misery, grief, despair—all the grim facts of human existence—for the extinction of which in the present life I am prescribing."

The Buddha's position has been well described by the noted Tibetan-trained Chinese scholar Garma C. C. Chang. In the *Buddhist Teaching of Totality* he has written:

Buddha was never [merely] a philosopher; His primary concern was to point out the way to liberation—liberation from the deep-rooted attachment to a delusory self which is the source of all passion-desires and their resultant pains and frustrations. Philosophical speculations were persistently rejected and denounced by Buddha as useless, foolish and unsalutary. Actually, in Buddha's teaching we do not find a philosophy; what we find is a significant therapeutic device, the instruction on how to get rid of the deep ego-clinging attitude.

Over and over again we hear the Buddha exhorting those who have come to him because they want relief from life's burdens and difficulties to keep their minds on the main goal: the destruction of that overweening separative ego through whose activities the world takes its unreal illusory form, thus preventing mankind from seeing the truth of life's *totality*; a wholeness to which each component part contributes—whether aware of it or not.

The Buddha constantly placed his emphasis on the necessity to face suffering (either real or imaginary) and to free oneself of it through the realization of the interpenetration of all existence, a blessed state attained by the destruction of every vestige of egocentrism. Here we see the teaching of a new approach to the nature of the self. In Buddhism the idea of the separate self, an "ego," is considered a mere intellectual invention, not a reality but simply a convenient term for designating an ever-changing combination, or bundle, of attributes known as *skandhas*.

*Skandhas*, in Buddhist thought, consist of forms, feelings, perceptions, mental formulations (ideas, wishes, dreams) and consciousness. The constant interplay and interconnection among the *skandhas* has the effect of giving a false sense of personal identity and continuity—whereas in truth there is no definite "I" existing by itself, independent of the ever-shifting relation among psychic and physical forces.

( The Buddha used the metaphor of a chariot to make this salient point. The word "chariot," he said, "does not indicate a simple, single reality; it is merely a descriptive term applied to a number of constituent parts placed in a certain relation to one another; and just as no part of this aggregate can be separated off and called a 'chariot,' so no part of the human creature can be set apart and called 'I.' " )

Difficult as this point of view may seem, it is not unknown to Western philosophic thought. William James, Schopenhauer, Berkeley and Bertrand Russell, among others, have expressed similar views. Most pertinent perhaps is the statement made by David Hume, the father of Western empiricism. Hume was expressing himself very much like a Buddhist when he wrote: "For my part when I enter most intimately into what I call *myself*, I always stumble on some particular perception or other, of heat or cold, light or shade, love or hatred, pain or pleasure. I can never catch myself at any time without a perception." Hume therefore concluded: "What we call the mind is nothing but a heap or bundle of different perceptions united together by certain relations," a concept interestingly similar to that of *skandhas*.

It might be useful here to point out a certain difference between Western and Buddhist philosophers which runs counter to any number of possible similarities in their approach to the basic question of being. In the mainstream of Western philosophic thought, a "philosopher's" theories and beliefs can be separated from his personal way of life and accepted as valid in themselves. By contrast, in the Buddha's view, to be worthy of the title of sage, a man must have striven to attain "awareness"—that favorite Buddhist word— and then, most important, act and live by what he has discovered to be true. The Dhammapada states: "A man who talks much of his teaching but does not practice it himself is like a cattleman counting another man's cattle. . . . Like beautiful flowers full of color, but without scent, are the well-chosen words of the man who does not act accordingly."

Buddhist teaching in relation to the true nature of the soul or self probably accounts in part for the allegation that it is a form of atheism. Actually, Buddhism is no more atheistic than it is theistic or pantheistic. The charge of atheism can hardly be laid at the door of a Teacher who could declare of the universe, or cosmos, in its wholeness (or *thusness*): "There is an unborn, an unoriginated, an unmade, an uncompounded. Were there not, O mendicants, there would be no escape from the world of the born, the originated, the made and the compounded."

Another stumbling block to the Westerner who approaches Buddhism is the charge that by emphasizing suffering, Buddhism becomes a religion of pessimism and despair; that its goal of nirvana, which appears to mean "extinction," can hardly be conducive to the living of a full and useful life.

As to nirvana, Buddhists reply that the term is to be somewhat differently interpreted than merely "extinction." What is extinguished on the attainment of nirvana is simply that self-centered, self-assertive life to which unenlightened man tends to cling as if it were the highest good and the final security. The truly "real" is not extinguished when nirvana is reached; rather, the real is then attained. Through the overcoming of the ego one is able to enter into communion with the whole universe; the horizon of the individual is extended to the very limits of reality, to a completely realized Oneness. Nirvana is not to be equated with existentialism's abyss of annihilation, but instead to a boundless expansion. The image should not be the drop of water which merges into the ocean and is lost but rather the ocean which enters into the drop.

There are two other frequently repeated words in early Buddhist teaching which have helped to add to the charge of gloom in Buddhism's view of life. One of these is the word *anicca*, the other is *dukkha*; they are closely related. *Anicca* stands for *impermanence*, a basic characteristic of existence which man either does not see or wishes not to see. The truth that all life is in a condition of transiency and flux is of course unarguable, yet even today the average man has not consciously assimilated this disturbing reality. Although continuous physical changes in the individual's body from infancy to childhood, through youth, maturity and old age, are plain to be seen, the constant minute alterations in the skin, cells and metabolic processes are less readily perceptible. In the

Buddha's view, human inability to recognize in the most intimate terms the inalienable laws of *anicca*, or impermanence, has helped to create man's fallacious belief in a fixed or permanent "self." And, in turn, this delusory belief in the fixed or permanent is one of the causes of *dukkha*, or suffering, for when we erroneously believe in enduringness we cannot accept the fact of impermanence and so we suffer.

It is not easy to accept the premise that one of life's basic conditions is inescapable suffering, true though this proves to be on even cursory examination. It may be helpful to consider another interpretation of the word *dukkha*: Literally it refers to an ill-made axle and therefore implies a wheel that is awry. *Dukkha* seen as awryness or out-of-kilterness clearly implies the possibility of correction.

⟨Certainly the Buddha, the world's first great psychologist, believed in the possibility of change. According to the Dhammapada, "All that we are is the result of our thoughts," and he went on to point out how thoughts can be subject to control through specific training and practice. He believed in the law of cause and effect and was at some pains to bring home to his followers the seriousness of this inexorable and inescapable pattern of life's activities: "I will teach you the law: *that* being present, *this* happens; from the arising of *that*, *this* arises; *that* being absent, *this* does not happen; from the cessation of *that*, *this* ceases." And here, of course we come to karma: "That which ye sow, ye reap," and a man even enters life, "reaper of the things he sowed," at another time and place. Karma is also, however, opportunity. Man, having had the rare good fortune to be born a human being and thus the possessor of special faculties and perceptions, can with the proper use of will and mind come to understand just who and where he is in the scheme of things.

Another charge laid at the door of Buddhism is its deficiency in "love." One of the most telling refutations of this charge can be found among the kindly, generous and cheerful people of predominantly Buddhist lands like Burma, Thailand and Tibet where alien influences were at a minimum until comparatively recent times. The belief that man is not an enduring entity, that he is, indeed, but a "process in time" seems to have cast little shadow on the spirits of these particular Buddhists; and against the accusation that the Theravadins have as their ideal the *arhat* who emphasizes individual enlightenment more than the *Bodhisattva* who stresses the enlightenment of all beings, one could place the fact that in many monasteries of the Theravada countries the day begins with prolonged and dynamic meditation on *metta*, or loving-kindness, a practice which is not to be approached mechanically or abstractly but as a vital outflowing current directed toward all life. (For more on the *metta* exercise, see pages 89–91.)

The *metta* meditation may well have its origin in the scripture known as *The Discourse on Universal Love*, in which the Buddha is quoted as saying: "As a mother, even at the risk of her own life, protects and loves her child, her only child, so let a man cultivate love without measure toward the whole world, above, below, and around, unstinted, unmixed with any feeling of differing or opposing interests. Let a man remain steadfastly in this state of mind all the while he is awake, whether he be standing, walking, sitting or lying down. This state of mind is the best in the world."

The Buddha himself is described in one of the old scriptures as personally undertaking the care of a sick and neglected monk, bathing and tending him as if he were his own child and chiding the neglectful brothers in words that have a curiously New Testament ring. "He who would wait on me, let him wait on the sick."

Yet even in his unfailing compassion the Buddha, ever the psychological realist, felt compelled to push the bereaved and bereft toward a new and larger consciousness as their one lasting and sure way to deal with personal pain. This is well illustrated in the story of Kisa Gotami, a young mother whose only and beloved child had died, leaving her almost out of her mind with grief and unable to accept the fact that the child was gone.

Having heard of the Great Teacher and miracle worker who was stopping at a place not far distant, she hastened to the Buddha and asked him to return her child to life. "Go first," said the Buddha, "to the village and ask the villagers for a handful of mustard seed and bring it to me here. This seed must, however, come from a house in which there has never been death." Kisa Gotami, still clasping her child's corpse in her arms, hurried eagerly to the village and went from house to house asking for the special mustard seed. In all her inquiries, however, she never found a house that had not been visited by death. When, at last, she could relate her own loss to the human lot, she relinquished her dead child for burial and returned to the Buddha to become his disciple.

This story is particularly characteristic of the Buddha's approach to individual sufferers. He had brought Kisa Gotami through her private grief to a sense of compassionate oneness with all life.

The Buddha's ministry lasted for more than forty years. In that time he wandered far and taught many people—courtesans, kings, farmers, skeptics and intellectuals. He had made a great concession, considering the social climate of the times, by admitting women into his Order (on the pleading, it is said, of his favorite disciple, the gentle Ananda). He had returned home to his family's palace for a visit, had converted his father and taken into his group of disciples his foster mother, his wife and his only son.

The Buddha's death came about, so legends tell us, as the consequence of his eating either poisonous mushrooms or pork that was spoiled—a meal he had taken at the invitation of a blacksmith named Cunda. It is entirely in character with the Buddha's egalitarian treatment of all people that he should have dined with a man of such low caste, and, in the Buddhist way, have accepted whatever he was offered as a repast. The word for the food he ate has been translated as "pig's soft food," but it is not clear whether it means the tender flesh of a pig or food eaten by pigs. Whatever it actually was, the stories which stress this circumstance agree that, although the Buddha accepted what had been prepared, he did ask his host not to serve it to the others who accompanied him but to bury it in a deep hole in the ground. Very soon after eating, the Buddha took sick. He controlled his violent pains in order that he might continue the journey he had undertaken as far as a certain river. Here he bathed and drank and, going to a nearby mango grove, "lay down on his right side in the attitude of a lion with one foot on the other." This was the same pose in which he was soon to die, a pose which can be seen today in a gigantic rock-hewn statue from the twelfth century lying in awesome quiet in the open green countryside at Polonnaruwa in Sri Lanka.

In character also with the Buddha's open and compassionate nature as expressed in these particular accounts of his departure from earth was his specific injunction to his faithful disciple Ananda that no one was to lay blame on Cunda, the blacksmith, for the unwholesome food he had innocently given the Buddha. It is related that special word was sent that he should feel no remorse for his unwitting deed. Quite the contrary, said the Buddha. "It was gain to thee, friend Cunda, great gain to thee that the *Tathagata** received his last alms from thee and attained Nirvana." Cunda's worthy action (giving the Buddha his last "alms") equaled in merit the maiden Sujata's deed, offering nourishing food at the time many years before, just prior to the Buddha's attainment of Supreme Enlightenment.†

After sending the reassuring message to Cunda, the Buddha went on across the river to a grove of sal trees and again lay down in "the lion's pose" from which he was not to rise again.

It has often been asserted that the account of the Buddha's eating pig or boar's meat is an outright fabrication—some say a legend perpetrated by Western scholars perhaps unwilling to accept the idea of the Buddha's Enlightenment. The basis for questioning this particular part of the story of the Buddha's *Parinirvana* is the fact that pig or boar's meat was regarded by all Indians of that time as unclean and unwholesome and would under no circumstances, or by anyone on whatever social level, have been offered to a respected teacher and an assembly of monks. In this view, the repast offered the Buddha would most certainly have been truffles, a highly regarded delicacy which unfortunately could be all too easily mistaken for a poisonous mushroom with a similar appearance.

It would be essentially un-Buddhist to devote too much space to different interpretations of the episode of the Buddha's death, but

* One of the titles for the Buddha, meaning "one who has come and gone this way."
† E. J. Thomas, *The Life of the Buddha as Legend and History*, Routledge & Kegan Paul, Ltd., London, 3rd ed., 1949.

another account of it reflects so interestingly on certain Buddhist doctrines that it calls for inclusion here. In this account, which has as its source a noted *sutra* of the Theravada School, the Parinirvana Sutra (Parinibbana Sutta) of the Digha Nikaya, the Buddha fully recovered after Cunda's meal (whatever it was). He had, however, "voluntarily promised to go into *Parinirvana* after a specified time provided that he had fulfilled his mission in this world and had no more justification to hang onto life. It was only after the Buddha had been reassured by the monks that he had nothing more to teach them that he announced his intention to enter *Parinirvana* within a given period. He did so to the dismay of Ananda, who realized too late that he had failed to request the Buddha to stay longer in the world for the benefit of suffering humanity."*

The most interesting point in this account lies in the emphasis it places on the quality of compassion. It was *out of compassion* that the Buddha—who had already attained nirvana long since— had continued to wander and preach "for the benefit of others," postponing indefinitely his *Parinirvana*, or final release from the world into which he had been born.

In this account, as in all others of the Buddha's demise, there is no difference of opinion, however, about the Buddha's composed and conscious end. As an Enlightened One he had attained complete mindfulness, a totally controlled consciousness which enabled him to leave his body in full possession of all his faculties. His last words were completely in character with the unique nature of his teaching, consonant with statements he had made on other occasions stressing man's own responsibility for his personal fate. "By one's self evil is done, by one's self one is purified. The pure and the impure stand and fall by themselves. No one can purify another." He asked that after his departure there be no fixed adherence to any rules except the simple basic premises, for he feared wisely that formalizing details of deportment and dogma would tend toward ossification and eventual schism within the *Sangha*. He asked that no one mourn his passing and reminded the weeping Ananda that decay is inherent in all physical phenomena. Serene

* From Lama Govinda in correspondence with the author.

and direct in these last moments, he exhorted his disciples, "Work with diligence. Be lamps unto yourselves. Betake yourselves to no external refuge. Look not for refuge to anyone beside yourself. Hold fast to the Truth as to a lamp."

So saying, there passed from the earthly scene a transcendent human being who, though born to an existence of ease and luxury, had spent more than half his lifetime wandering the roads of India, preaching a doctrine about a Way of Knowledge that all were welcome to follow, regardless of their past history or their present status in Indian society.

At his death the Buddha left behind a community of believers and a teaching destined, in spite of a number of inevitable mutations and vicissitudes, to become a world religion, one in which all sects, no matter what superficial distinctions are to be found among them, remain today still solidly grounded in the few relatively uncomplicated principles of belief and behavior first practiced and taught by the Buddha. Chief among these basic tenets is the acceptance of the truth that life involves impermanence and constant change (*anicca*). It also involves suffering (*dukkha*), owing to man's inability to accept impermanence as a basic law of existence; an inability related to the dominance of the ego with its unbridled appetites and anxieties. This dominating ego can, however, be transformed through practice in self-training (the Eightfold Path), which if faithfully followed will bring about drastic changes in consciousness, leading eventually to release from the irrational fear of loss and above all the fear of death or personal extinction.

The Buddhist disciple does not advance merely by accumulating innumerable good deeds but rather by increasing his understanding of his own nature and by learning to quell and transform those harmful and destructive tendencies which not only affect him personally but all life of which he is an integral part. A perfected Buddhist might be described as a human being who has reached a state in which moral training has become so deeply a part of his nature that it would be impossible for him to be involved in violence, cupidity, insensibility, low physical passion or other "unawarenesses." The word "sin" would not be appropriate here. It is ignorance, not fateful predilection as in the Christian sense of Original Sin, that concerns the Buddhist.

There seem to be substantial grounds for believing that the historic Buddha personally considered all ritual of any kind superfluous. At the beginning of his ministry he moved apart from the established rites of prayer and sacrifice and established nothing formal in their place. The earliest *Sangha* regulations contain no vows of obedience. They also indicate the absence of direct hierarchical rank other than pupil-teacher relations or simple seniority of membership in the *Sangha*. In time, to be sure, as it became necessary to establish some form of authority to handle increasing numbers of monks, hierarchies did grow up in Buddhist organizations in different countries. It has, however, been pointed out that Buddhism tended not to develop ranks of higher clergy with the power to dictate to lesser ranks all details of belief and religious observance.

Differences of opinion arose, naturally, as did also some disagreement among Buddhist followers, but, on the whole, ripples of dissension only lightly ruffled Buddhism's calm surface. They did not lead to violent schisms, to persecution and even death for alleged "heresy." It is specially noteworthy that in the long history of world Buddhism substantial differences of opinion on doctrine or procedures have led simply to the development and, significantly, the acceptance of different schools of thought rather than to sharply opposed, warring denominations. Although the basic original Buddhist teachings have remained constant in principle and intention, the individual disciple is seen as directly, personally involved in his own salvation, a point of view which allows exceptional latitude in matters of instruction and practice.

# Introduction
# to
# General
# Teaching
# and
# Practice

# The Asian Buddhist World

This map is designed only to give a general sense of the extent of the Asian Buddhist world and the geographic placement of certain key Buddhist sites. Some states, like Pakistan and Afghanistan, have been included because of their roles in Buddhist history or the presence within their boundaries of exceptional Buddhist art of the past—even if now mutilated.

Sea of Japan

KOREA

Kyoto

JAPAN

Yellow Sea

East China Sea

TAIWAN

South China Sea

PHILIPPINES

PACIFIC OCEAN

D O N E S I A

I n the first chapter the two major divisions within Buddhism were briefly noted. One of them, Hinayana, meaning "the Lesser (*hina*) Vessel" or "Vehicle" (*yana*), was a name given it by early followers of the Mahayana, or "Greater Vehicle of Salvation," not without some implied derogation on the part of the more expansive and permissive Mahayanists. As already mentioned, the term Theravada, or Way of the Elders, is now considered a more acceptable designation than Hinayana, although in general usage the latter term persists and often appears in Buddhist writing and oral instruction to indicate certain specific methods of practice as taught in this so-called Southern School which flourishes in such countries as Burma, Thailand and Sri Lanka.

As a part of Mahayana or Northern Buddhism, many centuries ago in the isolated fastnesses of "forbidden" Tibet there developed special forms of the Mahayana which are now beginning to take a strong place in contemporary Western Buddhism under the tutelage of transplanted teachers who fled their homeland after the Chinese invasion in 1958. The Tibetan tradition, known as Tantrayana or Vajrayana, is sometimes claimed to represent a separate Third School of advanced Buddhism. This claim does not meet with general agreement among other world Buddhists, who tend to consider Tantrayana, like Zen (also possessing unique attributes and of increasing interest to Westerners), as merely a special branch of the many-branched Mahayana. On the whole, Zen followers would appear to agree with this assessment, and it is noteworthy that Tibet's Dalai Lama has himself "strenuously" objected to speaking of Tibetan Buddhism as some special variant of Buddhism developed by Tibetans for Tibetans.*

Because the still generally accepted division of Buddhism into its two main branches, Mahayana and Hinayana (Theravada), seems consistently puzzling to Westerners, it might be helpful at the beginning of this section on general training and practice to borrow Christmas Humphrey's useful metaphor of an imaginary wheel whose hub is Hinayana and whose many spokes constitute the Mahayana. In this clarifying comparison the Hinayana hub is taken to represent what is sometimes referred to as the Old Wisdom School, or "original" Buddhism as first established in India and later in the Southeast Asian countries just mentioned—where its tenets are zealously followed today by a strong *Sangha*. From this central Hinayana hub of basic teachings—i.e., the Four Noble Truths and the Eightfold Path—there extend all the varied spokes of the Mahayana or so-called Northern School, whose geographic range includes northern India, Mongolia, Sikkim, Bhutan, Nepal, Vietnam, Cambodia, China, Korea and Japan.

A modern Zen roshi has suggested a further point of comparison between the two great divisions which also warrants careful consideration. In his view, Theravada emphasizes the humanity of the Buddha; Mahayana emphasizes the Buddha-nature of humanity. Whereas Theravada stresses the following of a moral life and high-principled behavior as the road to eventual Buddhahood, Mahayana inclines more toward tapping an intuitive wisdom to achieve the realization that one already possesses the Buddha-nature; it has simply to be "recovered" or uncovered, so to speak.

As an instance of Buddhism's generally harmonious interrelationships one might cite the World Synod held in Burma in 1953–1954 to commemorate the 2,500th birthday of the historic Buddha.

* Bhiksu Karma Khechong Sangpo, *Tibet Journal*, Vol. II, no. 3, Autumn, 1977.

This was allegedly the sixth of the Great Councils of Buddhism dating back to the first 250 years following the Buddha's death, when it is chronicled that the first four of these major Councils were convened with the purpose of reciting aloud and thus fixing in the minds of the *Sangha* members the contents of the *Tripitaka* (Three Baskets) of the Pali Canon. These three *Pitaka*—the word refers to the baskets in which palm-leaf manuscripts were stored—comprised first the rules of discipline for monks and nuns; second, collected discourses of the Buddha, anecdotes about his life; third, the *Abhidhamma* (also spelled *Abhidharma*), more abstruse scriptures dealing with—in modern, Western terms—psychology, philosophy and metaphysics.

After the Fourth Council, more than two thousand years elapsed before the Fifth, which, like the most recent one in this country, was also held in Burma, in Mandalay in the 1860s. At that time the agreed-upon Theravada texts were chiseled on hundreds of stone tablets erected by order of the devout Buddhist King Mindon. This chiseling in stone, although an act of conspicuous piety, seems far removed from the injunctions of the historic Buddha, who urged avoidance of dogmatic authoritarianism and, just prior to his death, assured his followers that they were free when he was gone to abolish all the lesser precepts of the Order if they so wished. This statement, like a number of others attributed to the Buddha, was obviously intended to discourage doctrinal hair-splitting and sectarianism. Unfortunately, it had in certain instances quite the opposite effect. It led some future *Sanghas* to call formal meetings to settle minor points of difference in doctrine and discipline—points which, one surmises, the Great Teacher had purposely left undefined.

Buddhists who attended the so-called Sixth Council in the 1950s in Rangoon met in conspicuous harmony. "Learned scholars from every possible school and part of the world participated in a new concordance of texts of the Tripitaka (the three baskets of the law)."* They convened in a specially constructed cavelike building, gathering for discussion in an eight-sided library (symbolic of the

* Lionel Landry, executive vice-president of the Asia Society of New York, in correspondence with the author.

Eightfold Path) donated by the Ford Foundation. In view of the fact that there were no reports of friction at this synod, it seems fair to assume that possible disagreements about such matters as which was the older or "truer" of the many texts and teachings of the two main schools, Hinayana and Mahayana, did not arise or at least caused no notable controversy. The question appears to be no longer pertinent to Buddhist practice—if, indeed, it ever was. Scholars may, and undoubtedly will, continue the debate (the vast field of Mahayana literature is as yet only partly explored), but Buddhism as a world religion remains relatively free of secular rigidity. It is still growing and expanding, making room for fresh cultural influences in conformity with the Buddha's wish to avoid fixed traditions of ritual and dogma.

In unequivocal words, accepted as coming straight from the Buddha, his followers were urged to develop their own perceptions: "Do not rely on what has been acquired by repeated hearing, nor upon tradition, nor upon rumor, nor upon what is in scripture, nor upon specious reasoning, nor upon another's seeming ability, nor upon the consideration, 'The monk is our teacher,' therefore to be believed. When you yourselves know: These things are good, these things are not blameable; these things are praised by the wise; when undertaken and observed, these things lead to benefit and happiness, enter on and abide in them."*

Statements of this kind quite naturally opened the way to that freedom of question and experiment which accounts for many of the seeming paradoxes one finds in Buddhism, in particular in the Mahayana School. These statements are also the source of some of the criticism which Mahayanists down the years have leveled at the Theravada, claiming that too rigid adherence to canonical rules through the many inevitable changes in man's consciousness and history can prove a hindrance to spiritual growth by preventing individuals or society from testing for themselves the truth of the Teaching.

To refer once again to the metaphor of the wheel, it seems plain

* Anguttaranikaya, Vol. I, ed. R. Morris, 2nd ed., 1961, Pali Text Society. Quoted in H. Saddhatissa, *The Buddha's Way*, New York, Braziller, 1971, p. 6.

that without both the hub (Hinayana) and the spokes (Mahayana) there would be no wheel. Taken together, they constitute the whole field of thought which developed not alone from the Buddha's sermons but also, down the years, from the minds of other profound Buddhist thinkers: Buddhaghosa, Vasubandhu, Nagarjuna —notably among many. It cannot be too often emphasized that Buddhism recognizes no sacred and revealed Scripture and no Divine Personality existing outside and beyond man and his world. In Buddhism there is no personalized single great Being whose final word is set forth in specific, sacred, never-to-be-questioned writings, as in the Judeo-Christian Bible. Buddhism is not a revealed faith but a religion of accumulated wisdom, and each generation is free to add to it without fear of the charge of heresy. It is essential to grasp this point if one hopes to acquire an understanding of the Buddhist Way.

In even a brief and oversimplified statement about Buddhism's generally accepted two main schools, it is impossible to avoid some mention of the development within each of a characteristic ideal, harmonious with its teaching.

The Hinayana ideal is embodied in the Sanskrit term *arhat* (in Pali, *arahat* or *arahant*) already mentioned. The *arhat* is a Buddhist follower who by his own strenuous endeavors has reached the stage of enlightenment; has attained nirvana. The real meaning of being an *arhat* has been described in simple and explicit terms by a noted Burmese Hinayanist, U Thittila: "The extinction of greed, the extinction of anger, the extinction of delusion—this is indeed called *Nibbana* [*Nirvana*]. And for the disciple thus freed [i.e., the *Arhat*], in whose heart dwells peace, there is nothing to be added to what has been done and naught more remains for him to do."

In other words, the *arhat* has attained nirvana without, however, leaving the earthly plane, for in this Hinayana conception nirvana is merely the extinction of false ideas, in particular the hard-to-conquer belief in a separate ego. With the overcoming of the illusion of "separateness" there is also overcome the illusion of birth and death which arises directly from the mistaken and limiting notion of an individual self. To repeat once more: in the great cyclic totality there is no *self* and no *other*; the two are recognized as differing aspects of one whole.

With the development of the Mahayana there arose a somewhat different ideal from that of the *arhat*: the compassionate *Bodhisattva*. This ultimate model of the Mahayanists implies another perception of an enlightened being. The *Bodhisattva* undertakes responsibility not only for his own liberation but for all life. Having reached the goal of nirvana he, in a sense, "postpones" his own release from the world in order to give aid to all life not yet aware of Enlightenment. This goal finds expression in the Bodhisattva Vow, as chanted in the daily litany of the Mahayanist monks and nuns:

> Sentient beings are numberless;
> I vow to save them all.
> Delusions are inexhaustible;
> I vow to end them all.
> The gates of the Dharma* are manifold;
> I vow to enter them all.
> The Buddha-way is supreme;
> I vow to complete it.

If the ascetic, monastic Hinayanists, journeying on what Heinrich Zimmer has called the Little Ferryboat, are sometimes described as solitary travelers who, following the Master's injunction to "act as lights unto themselves," must steer the difficult strait of individual release essentially on their own, by contrast Mahayana in offering its Large Ferryboat to the Other Shore, would appear to be striving to accommodate everyone. This significant shift of emphasis rises from the recognition that men are obviously living at different stages of spiritual development and therefore each seeker should be helped to follow whatever method appears best suited to his individual needs or lying within his particular range of comprehension.

---

* *Dharma:* This Sanskrit term of wide meaning depends for its specific interpretation on the context in which it is used. Here it might be said to represent Buddhist teaching.

The Buddha's original teaching was conducted by way of preaching and subsequent discussion; nothing was written down. The basic principles were, however, formally memorized, as we have seen, and a fundamental substructure remained through all the inevitable changes as Buddhism moved north, south and west from India along the great trade routes and oasis cities.

( During this prolonged period of expansion, Buddhism infiltrated many cultures and absorbed unfamiliar influences. It should, therefore, come as no surprise to encounter, in the permissive, far-wandering Mahayana, types of worship that seem unrelated to early Buddhist teaching. In various sects and schools of the Mahayana, one finds proliferation not only of Buddhas and *Bodhisattvas* of varying significance and with different attributes but also complicated pantheons of such minor deities as Guardians of the Four Directions, Serpent Kings, wrathful demons, assorted nature spirits and so on, each "manifestation" accompanied by the inevitable altars, rosaries, gongs, bells, incense, prayer wheels, *mantras, thankas, mudras,* and *asanas* representative of the ritual-loving and mythmaking proclivities of mankind and the resultant art of religious expression)

The growth of the *Bodhisattva* ideal has a special significance important to recognize because it indicates a subtle change which gradually took place in Buddhist thought, giving more formal emphasis to active compassion (*karuna*) in addition to transcendental wisdom (*prajna*). During the gradual geographical spread of Mahayana Buddhism, the *Bodhisattva* as a model became steadily more influential, until eventually there arose devotional sects in which salvation was assured by the mere pronouncing of a sacred name or phrase, as exemplified in Pure Land Buddhism with its worship of the mythological Amida Buddha, a type of devotion encapsulated in Japan today in the familiar invocation *Namu Amida Butsu* (*Nembutsu*). Invocations of this nature need not indicate merely mindless formulas employed by simple followers of Buddhism. To the invoker with developed understanding they possess a profound inner significance. In the utterance of Nembutsu, for example, concentration on the Buddha within as a means of attaining spiritual unity is implied, and the common

Tibetan chant *Om mani padme hum*, usually but somewhat inadequately translated as "Hail to the Jewel in the Lotus," is a powerful esoteric *mantra* (associated with the *Bodhisattva* of Compassion, Avalokiteshvara), which contains "the primordial sound of the universe." This mantra has been extensively analyzed by Lama Anagarika Govinda in *Foundations of Tibetan Mysticism*.

When it comes to consideration of proper Buddhist daily conduct, generalizations about the contrast between the followers of the *arhat* ideal and that of the *bodhisattva* tend to break down. "Helping one's fellows," clearly a basic part of Hinayanists' everyday practice, is attested to in a number of engaging accounts of daily life in Theravada countries. Among these accounts two books about life in Burma stand out. One is H. Fielding Hall's *The Soul of a People*. The other is Sir George Scott's delightful memoir *The Burman: His Life and Notions*, which he wrote under the pseudonym of Shway Yoe. Scott, an eminent British civil servant, describes the daily existence, at the end of the nineteenth century, of a warm-hearted, generous, friendly people imbued with the spirit of Buddhist brotherliness which, to be sure, did not exclude the gathering of "merit" for brotherly deeds. If a Burman built a little bridge over a stream to keep the traveler from wetting his feet, if he placed pots of cool water on a shaded platform before his house to allay the thirst of any passer-by, he could follow these meritorious small acts by a visit to the local pagoda, where he could strike a bronze bell and utter a significant invocation, "May all who hear this sound share in the merit my deed has earned." Such inclusiveness seems effectively to contradict any charge that the Hinayanist is, in practice, more self-centered than the Mahayanist.

Plainly, Buddhism from its earliest history emphasized the necessity of helping others, an example given by the Buddha himself in the pivotal hour of choice when he faced the responsibility and

*A famous wooden figure of the Buddha of the Future, Maitreya (Miroku, in Japanese). Seventh century* A.D. *Nara, Japan.*

*Amida or Amitabha Buddha (the Buddha of the Pure Land Sect) descending from his Western Paradise, accompanied by Bodhisattvas. A favorite theme in formal Japanese religious art. Thirteenth–fourteenth century.*

inevitable difficulties of going forth to teach what he understood as the way to deliverance. This momentous selfless decision was amplified later by his establishment of teaching groups among his disciples.

There are a number of further subtleties in the two seemingly contradictory ideals described above. One which should be mentioned is that the concept of a Savior, of "salvation through intercession," is not considered entirely the correct interpretation of the *Bodhisattva* role. Helpfulness to others is, in Buddhism, significantly not equated with the idea, "I am my brother's keeper." Instead Buddhism teaches "I am my brother." This all-important key to Buddhist practice expresses that essential unity or oneness of all life taught by the historic Buddha.

Buddhism's singular flexibility in the matter of dogma has permitted it, during the more than 2,500 years of its existence, to follow many paths of philosophy, metaphysics, mysticism, psychology and sociology, as well as what today we call science. Since Buddhism is rooted in human rather than divine reality, it follows that it is free in theory (if not in practice) to reject any claims that the original purity or truth of a religion may be lost in the travels and changes of its historical development. By the very nature of the Great Teacher's own precepts, Buddhism escaped the constricting bonds of sacrosanct spiritual authority; as also— since it was never confined within the parameters of a fixed world cosmology—it has been spared many of the problems that orthodox Christian and Jewish theologians must face in the present Space Age.

For it is unfortunately true that the universe with which contemporary astrophysics confronts the modern mind bears very little relationship to Western man's religions as taught in established churches. Raised in the belief in an anthropomorphic Father God whose sacred Law is contained in scriptures replete with contradictions and irrelevancies, where every word is nonetheless declared by eminent divines to be "true," Western man has understandably reacted in either shocked disbelief or self-protective indifference to scientific reports on the awesome nature of the cosmos. Multiple island universes, the possibility of intelligent life in other solar systems, the presence of black holes in space, antimatter and innumerable other mysteries of stellar phenomena so stun and confound him that he turns away in fear and confusion.

This particular existential dilemma has been successfully bypassed by Buddhism. For centuries it has taught that there are many more worlds than one, that man lives in the midst of any number of interactive "systems," ethereal as well as visible. The Buddha, in attempting to stretch the minds of his disciples to encompass the stupendous dimensions of the universe, made use of an old Hindu term, *kalpa*, which designates the truly indescribable duration of time stretching between an initial condensation of a world system and its final dissolution or, in Indian mythological terminology, the space between the "in-breath and the out-breath of Brahma, the Creator."

Try to imagine, said the Buddha to his followers,* a mountain higher than the highest peak in the Himalayas. Now imagine a man coming just once every one hundred years to this stone mountain in order to touch it with the softest and sheerest piece of gauze, like the most delicate of fabrics made in Benares. The time it would take such a man to wear away that entire mountain would equal about the extent of a *kalpa*.

This graphic image makes a direct impact on the mind, touching the imagination far more directly than any abstract phrase about light-years. The inconceivable number of digits representing the distance light travels in one year is reckoned at 5,878,000,000,000 miles. This, of course, is a figure of such dimension that the ordinary brain cannot adequately deal with it. The Buddha's metaphor of the Himalayan peak and the man with a piece of fine silk gauze may seem equally stupefying in its suggestion of the duration of a *kalpa*, but it is at least more directly perceptible.

The extraordinary thing is that in spite of their awareness, their calm acceptance of the overwhelming vastness and intricacy of the universe, Buddhists long ago seemed able to reconcile them-

* *Buddhism: Its Essence and Development*, Edward Conze, Oxford, Bruno Cassirer, 1951, p. 49. *Three Ways of Asian Wisdom*, N. W. Ross, New York, Simon and Schuster, 1966, pp. 64–65.

selves to this incredible immensity while also believing in the meaningfulness of *personal* discipline and the refining of a man's *individual* nature. Buddhism taught, and still teaches, that the total universe and its total consciousness are directly affected by our freeing ourselves from the distortions of self-centeredness through developing human *mindfulness*. On this minor planet, Earth, whose relative cosmic importance could be described as "like a single grain of sand in all the sands of the Ganges River," the All-Enlightened Buddha dared to ask individual man to become wholly awake and aware. One can hardly imagine a more prodigious personal challenge!

The aim of achieving awareness of the subtle interaction and interpenetration of all things one with another in a complete harmony, of acquiring the sense of an ever self-creating, infinite life, a "universal communion" without beginning or end, underlies—it may be safely said—all Buddhist meditative exercises and practices, no matter what the sect. Nonetheless, *different symbols and disciplines may be employed to bring about this state of consciousness*.

For example, to illuminate the harmonious interplay and interconvertibility of all forms of life within the Absolute, one Mahayana form of Buddhism in Japan, the Kegon, uses the vivid symbol of Indra's Net. This great imaginary net, which significantly bears the name of one of the major deities of old India, is to be visualized —meditated upon—as stretching throughout the entire universe: its vertical extension representing time; its horizontal, space. At every point where the net's threads interconnect, one imagines a crystal bead symbolizing an individual existence. Each one of these innumerable individual crystal beads reflects on its surface not only every other bead in the net but every reflection of every other bead, thus creating numberless, endless reflections of each other while forming one complete and total *whole*.

The American-born woman who became an abbess of a Japanese temple, Ruth Fuller Sasaki, in a small informative book* written

* *Zen: A Religion*, The First Zen Institute of America, New York, 1958.

for the layman some years ago, tells us that in Zen a quite different and much simpler symbol is used to illustrate the totality of the universe in time and space. Zen's symbol is that of a single flower once held up to view by the preaching Buddha as a wordless message to his listeners. In all the attentive congregation there was only one disciple who immediately caught the Buddha's meaning. This was Mahakasyapa, or simply Kasyapa, who became "Maha," or Great, Kasyapa owing to his insight. When Kasyapa smiled a special smile of comprehension at the sight of the blossom in his Teacher's hand, the Buddha offered him the flower and with it the tacit honor of transmitting the Great Teaching of "the Whole," that single unity or totality which silently expresses itself, and may be fully apprehended in any of its diverse parts.

Among Western poets, many have given expression to a comparable sense of the interrelated oneness of the universe. One thinks immediately of those lines of Francis Thompson:

> . . . thou canst not stir a flower
> without troubling of a star.

There is also the often-quoted stanza from William Blake:

> To see a World in a Grain of Sand
> And a Heaven in a Wild Flower,
> Hold Infinity in the palm of your hand
> And Eternity in an hour.

John Donne, the seventeenth-century English poet and preacher, stated in one of his sermons, "God is so omnipresent . . . that God is an angel in an angel, and a stone in a stone and a straw in a straw." There are, in short, any number of literary luminaries from our part of the world who have written lines expressing in their own terms the Buddha's metaphor of a single flower which can symbolize life's infinite diversity and all-embracing unity.

A specific exposition of how to recognize, in personal terms, this universal interrelatedness was given by one of Ruth Fuller Sasaki's Japanese priest-instructors:

Now think about yourself. You think you are a separate and independent individual. But you are not. Without your father and mother you would not be. Without their fathers and mothers, your father and mother would not have been and you would not be. . . . And so we can go back endlessly to the origin of the human race and before that and before that. You, at this moment, are the apex of the great triangle formed by all these previous individual lives.* In you they all exist today. They live in you today as truly as they lived individually in what we call time.

But, in addition, just as you live today by virtue of all the other individuals and existences in the world at this moment—your body is sustained by the food cultivated and processed by innumerable persons throughout the present world, your body is covered by clothing produced by innumerable persons throughout the present world, your activities are conditioned by the activities of innumerable persons living in the present world, your thinking is conditioned by the thinking of innumerable persons living in the present world—so the bodies, the actions, the thinking of all your ancestors who form the great triangle of which you are the present apex, have in their turn been dependent upon and conditioned by the innumerable persons existing in the world at the time they individually lived. So, if we consider that all past time is concentrated in you at this moment, we must also consider that all past space is also concentrated in you at this moment. Therefore you and every other being in the world at this instant actually each stand at the apex of a great cone rather than a triangle.

But this is not all. From you will come your children and their children's children; from your actions will come the results of your actions and the results of those results; and from your thoughts will

* A recent piece on genealogical research in the *New York Times*, July 25, 1976, stated that "in the course of 21 generations a person accumulates one million ancestors!"

*A favorite theme of Buddhist artists everywhere is the* Bodhisattva, *an evolved human being who postpones his own Nirvana to aid all life in the quest for enlightenment. This example: Avalokiteshvara Padmapani ("Lotus in Hand"), painted on a wall in the famous Ajanta caves in India, circa 600–642* A.D. *A tender though detached princely figure, significantly holding a long-stemmed flower.*

come the future thinking and the thinking resulting from that thinking, *ad infinitum*. You hold within yourself the seed from which the future will spring. Just as much as you at this moment are the entirety of past time, so you are the entirety of future time. Just as you at this moment represent the concentration of all past space, so you at this moment represent the concentration of all space in the future. And this is true for each sentient or non-sentient existence in the universe. In you and in each one of them at this moment is all time and all space. In other words, this moment is all.*

Out of this kind of teaching there have inevitably sprung certain Buddhist characteristics of infinite gratitude to the past and to the present and—as part of this gratitude—determination to give service to all life and accept responsibility for the future. This blend of wisdom (*prajna*) and compassion (*karuna*) finds explicit expression in those famous Four Vows repeated daily by many thousands of Buddhist monks of the Mahayana School, as quoted on page 48.

* *Zen: A Religion*, pp. 15–17.

Two Buddhist beliefs which seem particularly to attract and sometimes disturb Western minds are the theories of *karma* and reincarnation. The idea expressed in the familiar saying of St. Paul, "Whatsoever a man soweth that shall he also reap," is basic to most religious thought, including Christianity. It was early incorporated into Buddhism, where it fitted into the framework of the generally accepted Asian theory of reincarnation or rebirth. In the simplest terms, reincarnation is the theory that each human being lives more than one life. The law of karma can be considered a corollary of this theory of rebirth, in the sense that each individual existence reflects the karmic effect of a former state. In Buddhism, as we shall see, however, an individual can free himself from his past by intention. It has been said that the only miracle Buddhism admits is a change of heart; otherwise we would never be liberated from the past, which is infinite.

Sir Edwin Arnold, the British poet (1832–1904) whose long epic poem about the Buddha's life and teaching, *The Light of Asia*, was so widely read and influential at the time it was written, has defined karma in four lines of verse:

> Karma—all that total of a soul
> Which is the things it did, the thoughts it had,
> The "Self" it wove—with woof of viewless time
> Crossed on the warp invisible of acts. . . .

Further on, in the section on Tantrism, we shall find this simile of the warp and woof recurring. At this point it need only be repeated that the strictly personal view of rebirth is not the view of developed Buddhist thought. In Buddhism, it must be remembered, the ego is not considered an entity but rather a process in time. The aggregate of psychophysical energies which make up the individual personality or self as it appears to exist in a practical or moral sense in everyday life does not constitute in Buddhism a "soul" in any metaphysical interpretation of the word.

*A lotus pod as representative of the Buddhist use of a single symbol to express the interrelated oneness of the universe.*

In an illuminating foreword to his translation of the Tibetan Book of the Dead, which will be discussed at some length in the section on Tibetan teachings, the noted British scholar W. Y. Evans-Wentz has not only shed interesting light on the matter of Buddhism's true position on the laws of karma, he has also quoted a surprising but relevant passage on karma and heredity, by the great nineteenth-century British scientist Thomas Huxley, in his book *Evolution and Ethics.* Since heredity (in spite of divided modern opinion on its significance and influence) is a term familiar to Westerners, Dr. Huxley's attempt to link the ideas of karma and heredity will be included here to serve as a possible bridge between two seemingly unrelated ways of thought.

In *Evolution and Ethics* Dr. Huxley wrote:

Everyday experience familiarizes us with the facts which are grouped under the name of heredity. Every one of us bears upon him obvious marks of his parentage, perhaps of remoter relationships. More par-

ticularly, the sum of tendencies to act in a certain way, which we shall call "character," is often to be traced through a long series of progenitors and collaterals. So we may justly say that this "character"—this moral and intellectual essence of a man—does veritably pass over from one fleshly tabernacle to another, and does really transmigrate from generation to generation. In the new-born infant, the character of the stock lies latent, and the Ego is little more than a bundle of potentialities. But, very early, these become actualities; from childhood to age they manifest themselves in dullness or brightness, weakness or strength, viciousness or uprightness; and with each feature modified by confluence with another character, if by nothing else, the character passes on to its incarnation in new bodies. The Indian philosophers called character, as thus defined, "karma." . . . In the theory of evolution, the tendency of a germ to develop according to a certain specific type, e.g. of the kidney bean seed to grow into a plant having all the characteristics of *Phaseolus vulgaris*, is its karma. It is the last inheritor and the last result of all the conditions that affected a line of ancestry which goes back for many millions of years, to the time when life first appeared on earth.

Then quoting Professor T. W. Rhys-Davids, Huxley ends: ". . . the snowdrop [a flower] is a snowdrop and not an oak, and just that kind of snowdrop, because it is the outcome of the karma of an endless series of past experiences."

In summation, and at the risk of repetitiousness, one should stress that in Buddhist teaching, karma is not seen as a blind implacable determinism, even though it includes such apparently irrevocable factors as one's family and circumstances of birth, over which an individual would appear to have no control whatever. Buddhism asserts that in reality there is no such thing as chance or fate; this idea is even carried as far as the belief held by

*High in the cliffs of Afghanistan, at Bamiyan, stand the colossal remains of a Buddha, one of many rock-hewn images in this region lying along the old trade routes that brought not only merchants and traders but, from the 4th century* A.D. *on, awe-struck Chinese pilgrims visiting holy India, the Buddha's homeland. Unfortunately, many of these images were mutilated by fanatic alien invaders. Fourth–fifth century* A.D.

some sects that each soul on its many-lived journey *chooses* its own parents. Moreover, each moment that we live today has been brought into being by past actions, and just as inevitably each moment of the future will be determined by the so-called present. What then keeps man from being a mere helpless pawn of his destiny? It is his own free will. As a human being man has, through his unique gift of will and his heightened (though often neglected) powers of perception, the chance to alter his behavior and thus his life situation.

In Buddhism it is ignorance, not sin, that gives man his difficulties, and ignorance can, by specific *teachable* techniques, be modified, even overcome. One has only to make the right effort! This is a key point worth repeating. Blame and guilt play no part in Buddhism; shame, however, over personal inadequacies can be a significant aspect of an individual's transformation.

Self-knowledge is the one sure, indisputable path by which we can extricate ourselves from the brambles of conditioned life. The Dhammapada states: "All that we are is made up of our thoughts." From this it would follow that since thoughts are subject to control, it is quite possible to alter one's attitude, an alteration that can drastically change an individual's life. This whole process is, however, much less simple than the mere exercise of mind over matter, as we hope to establish in the following pages.

# Three Specific Approaches to Buddhism

There are, as has already been made abundantly clear, many ways of teaching and practicing Buddhism. The three chapters that follow will consider three of these approaches. Whatever their differences in outer form, they share a common inner intention.

The first of these ways lies in the Theravada tradition associated with Southeastern Asia, in particular with the countries of Sri Lanka, Thailand and Burma.

The other two, Tantrayana (also called Vajrayana) and Zen—today respectively associated with Tibet and Japan—have grown, as already pointed out, from the many-spoked Mahayana of Buddhism's northern and far eastern migrations.

These three methods of practice have been selected because at the present time they are attracting increasing numbers of students and are having a significant cultural effect on the West.

# Theravada
# or Hinayana
# Buddhism

Any account of the rise of Hinayana Buddhism in Southeast Asia, and specifically on the important island of Sri Lanka—the home of the Buddhist Canon as first written in Pali and thus generally acknowledged as the fountainhead of the School's teaching—must of necessity begin with the famous proselytizing Indian Emperor Ashoka (264–226 B.C.). The conversion to the Buddhist faith of Ashoka, one of the most remarkable men of all time, is considered as important to Buddhism in Asia as the conversion of Constantine the Great* was to Christianity in the West.

Ashoka was the grandson of Chandragupta, another powerful Indian ruler of the third century B.C., who, when still only an insignificant army officer, demonstrated exceptional military genius and brilliant opportunism by taking immediate advantage of the death of Alexander the Great, the daring Macedonian who had invaded India's northwestern provinces some years before. Chandragupta reacted to the news of Alexander's demise in a distant land by swiftly and fiercely attacking the Indian settlements of this earlier Mediterranean invasion. When these colonies were overcome, Chandragupta went on to other astounding military triumphs

* Constantine was a Roman emperor (A.D. 306–337) who adopted the Christian faith and became one of its most zealous advocates.

which made it possible for him to establish firm rulership over a vast part of India.

This great domain passed to Chandragupta's son, the peaceful Bindusara. Little is known of this monarch's activities, but a story does survive that he once expressed the wish to "purchase" a philosopher from the Greeks and was told that it was not their custom to sell their philosophers, an anecdote which has been taken to indicate that Bindusara possessed an "inquiring mind." If true, this characteristic was destined to come to full flower in the life of his son Ashoka.

At the beginning of his career, Ashoka gave little indication of his future role as a wise and compassionate ruler. With a ruthlessness and vigor equal to his grandfather's, he set out to enlarge the kingdom he had inherited. Among the many bloody wars Ashoka waged, one of the most merciless was against the neighboring kingdom of Kalinga, during which, so the records tell us, one hundred thousand people were slain, fifty thousand carried into captivity and countless others left to die of famine and disease.

It is generally accepted that this wholesale slaughter and destruction of an entire kingdom changed the course of Ashoka's life, turning him from a ruthless conqueror into a peaceful monarch motivated by the highest moral principles. The exact details of this tremendous change of direction on Ashoka's part are not easily established, although the record of the change itself is unquestionably set forth in the famous imperial Rock Edicts engraved at his order on the faces of boulders and specially erected stone pillars throughout his vast kingdom. It is of course quite conceivable, as Professor Trevor Ling has suggested in his valuable book *The Buddha*, that Ashoka's change of heart came about simply as the outcome of his own mature reflections, perhaps due to the influence of a new sense of social ethics with which Buddhism had been subtly infiltrating the Indian consciousness for some two centuries.

*Lion-crowned column at Lauriya Nandangarh, India, erected by the Indian emperor Ashoka, the monarch who sent Buddhist teachers far and wide in the Asian world. Third century* B.C.

Although Ashoka as a young prince had been educated in the strictest Brahmin tradition of correct kingly behavior, he could hardly have been unaware of teachings with a quite different emphasis then stirring in his land. The orthodox Brahminical idea of proper kingly behavior had been conceived of in terms of *personal dharma*, the meticulously correct performance of monarchical duties, including the expansion of the boundaries of one's kingdom by force if necessary. In place of this working out of *personal dharma* in rulership, the Buddhists conceived of a king as the instrument of a higher and *universal Dharma*, or Law, under which —without use of force—all men would learn that it was possible to live in harmony. The importance of this change of view cannot be overestimated.

What, if any, direct role members of the Buddhist *Sangha* played in Ashoka's altered behavior has also never been clearly established. His transformation was probably gradual, in consonance with the measured pattern of Buddhist teaching. There is a story of Ashoka summoning to his court, "for instruction," a noted Buddhist teacher who was then living in a far off forest retreat. Traveling a long

distance by rivers and over land, with a few Buddhist companions, this dedicated monk arrived in due course at Ashoka's capital (the modern city of Patna), where he "consecrated" the emperor to Buddhism. After this ceremony, the emperor, his entire court and the visiting monks set out on a pilgrimage to the Buddha's birthplace at Lumbini. Here he set up what is known as the Second Minor Rock Edict, on which he testified that in the twentieth year of his reign, he, Ashoka, "came in person and reverenced the place where Buddha Shakyamuni was born" and at that time "caused a stone enclosure to be made and a stone pillar to be erected."

Ashoka's acceptance of Buddhism was, as already noted, an event of inestimable importance to the Asian world. As head of both Church and State, a position of supreme power, he was able to propagate the Buddhist faith far and wide. To the uttermost reaches of his vast Indian kingdom, and well beyond, he sent missionaries preaching a new doctrine: peaceful rather than warlike solutions for problems, the essential brotherhood of all living things, the necessity of compassion and strenuous personal endeavor in every individual life.

It is Ashoka who, in effect, may be credited with having made Buddhism a world religion. Not only did he use rocks and pillars as a way of preserving the teachings of Buddhism and the record of his royal efforts on Buddhism's behalf,* but he sent envoys incredible distances into strange lands and unfamiliar cultures: as far as Egypt under Ptolemy II, Syria under Antiochus II, and other parts of the Mediterranean and Aegean worlds.

Ashoka's Buddhism has been well described as practical morality backed by his own personal example. As Supreme Ruler he lived the life of a faithful Buddhist, even to the abjuring of meat at the palace table. Toward his own subjects he set an example of unparalleled generosity and good will: building hospitals, reservoirs, wells; maintaining good roads and wayside inns in remote areas; ordering medical aid for animals as well as people—all this in the third century B.C. He was the first, if not the only, all-powerful

---

* *The Edicts of Ashoka*, Vincent A. Smith, London, 1909 (rare book out of print). *The History of Aryan Rule in India from the Earliest Times to the Death of Akbar*, E. B. Havell, New York, no date.

emperor in history to make himself totally accessible to his subjects and their needs and wishes. One of the most famous of the many formal records, to which we owe so much of our general information about Ashoka and his period, states categorically that the emperor is available to anyone with a problem at any time— "whether I am dining, or in the ladies' apartments, or in my bedroom, or in my closet, or in my carriage, or in the palace gardens."

An important island off the southern tip of India, today's Sri Lanka, was the scene of Ashoka's most significant and successful missionary endeavor. According to legend, King Tissa, the ruler of this island kingdom so long known to the West as Ceylon, once sent Ashoka a gift of the most precious pearls to be found in the waters of his homeland. In return, the Indian emperor sent back the most precious gift he had to offer: the teachings of the Buddha. Buddhism was conveyed to the island by the emperor's son (some legends say his younger brother) Mahendra or Mahinda, who, relinquishing his royal rights to an Indian throne, set off joyfully to teach Buddhism to the people of this distant southern kingdom.

Mahendra was followed to Sri Lanka, so we are told, by the princess-nun Sanghamitta, the emperor's only daughter and, some stories allege, the heir to her father's throne. With her on her journey Sanghamitta is believed to have taken a branch of the Bodhi Tree from northern India under which the Buddha attained Enlightenment. The great pipal tree which can be seen to this day in the still impressive ruins of the one-time glorious capital city of Anuradhapura is believed to have grown from the very cutting delivered by the princess in the third century B.C. (Since local records testify to the tree's presence on this site for well over two thousand years, and as pipal trees are known to live for many centuries, there may be truth in the claim that this is, indeed, the oldest known historical tree in the world.)

In Theravada countries, the great Buddhist monasteries have always played a notably relevant role in national life. In these lands it is still considered a vital part of a young layman's education for him to spend a period of his early life in a monastery undergoing training similar to that given fellow countrymen who expect at maturity to assume the habit and tonsure of monkhood.

To this day, in spite of the cultural impact of Western invasions, both subtle and direct, it is commonplace for Buddhist laymen, on every level of Southeast Asian life, to retire regularly to some Buddhist monastery for meditation or retreat. A British admiral who took a course in a specific type of Buddhist mind-training a few years ago in a monastery outside Rangoon found among his fellow "monks" the chief of the Rangoon police and the owner of a flourishing chain of sterilized-milk factories.

Attesting to the strength of this early monastic experience are such modern Theravadin laymen as U Nu, the colorful and dynamic former Premier of Burma, who, in his days of power, was dubbed by Western journalists "the Prime Minister who meditates" (an activity which plainly set him apart from his Western counterparts), and U Thant, the modest Burmese educator who, as a much-honored Secretary General of the United Nations, was known to continue faithfully with disciplined meditation, no matter what the demands of his worldly position.*

In Thailand the present king, Bhumipol Adulyadej, widely known (among other distinguishing characteristics) as a serious-minded jazz buff, spent a specific period as a Buddhist *bhikkhu* (monk) preparing for his role as hereditary protector of Buddhism in his country. This modern monarch's most noted predecessor was the gifted nineteenth-century ruler King Mongkut, made familiar to the West through theater and film productions of *The King and I*, based on sensationalized accounts of Siamese court life taken in part from the diaries of a Victorian governess whom Mongkut had hired to teach his children English.

In a lively and well-researched monograph, *King Mongkut of Siam*, A. B. Griswold, an authority on Thai history and art, presents this remarkable personality in a fresh and, one assumes, more

---

* Something of the distinctively Buddhist qualities brought to his exacting post by U Thant have been vividly described by an admiring colleague, Robert Muller, in his book: *Most of All They Taught Me Happiness*, Doubleday, 1978; also in *U Thant: The Search for Peace* by June Bingham, Knopf, 1966; and in the *Bulletin of the United Nations Meditation Group*, November, 1974, dedicated to U Thant.

accurate perspective. Far from being, in Griswold's words, the "musical clown" or the "irrational despot" that these successful theatrical ventures might suggest, Mongkut was in reality a distinguished and enlightened monarch, very much in the tradition of that preeminent Indian Buddhist ruler of the distant past, the Emperor Ashoka. For this reason some reappraisal of Mongkut's character seems not inappropriate in any consideration of Theravada Buddhism as practiced in Thailand.

Although he was the rightful heir to the Siamese throne, Mongkut, born in 1804, was, on his father's sudden death, bypassed by the State Council in favor of a half-brother whose lineage on his mother's side was less exalted than Mongkut's. Without opposing the Council's choice, which could of course have precipitated civil disorder, Mongkut calmly remained on in the peace and quiet of the meditative monastic life he had been living for some years. This decision to continue a monkish existence rather than fight for his princely rights might have seemed the worst possible preparation for assuming eventual kingship. On the contrary, it proved of inestimable value to the future monarch. He used it, Griswold tells us, as an opportunity to develop "an acute sense of reality and a knowledge of people he could not possibly have got amid the artificialities of palace life."

Griswold's development of this particular theme gives an illuminating picture of life in a Theravada monastery in the nineteenth century. It seems well worth quoting for what it tells us not only of the behavior patterns of Theravada monks in the immediate past but even as they exist in the present.

The monkhood is a startlingly democratic institution. Its members are drawn from all levels of society, and distinctions of rank depend on function and seniority rather than birth or worldly position. To follow the Discipline strictly, the monks must not only abstain from stealing, lying and idle talk, taking life, handling money, indulgence in sex, intoxicants, luxuries and frivolous amusements; they must also obey no less than 227 rules that govern all the minutiae of daily conduct and manners. They can have no possessions except the yellow robe, the alms-bowl, and a few personal necessaries. They get their food by going forth in the morning, traveling with downcast eyes on foot along the road or by canoe in the canals, pausing when signaled by a householder who offers to fill their alms-bowl.

Although Mongkut, when he was living as a monk, belonged to an ostensibly meditative order, this did not prevent him from leading an active physical life. He made long, arduous pilgrimages to different parts of his future kingdom, acquiring thereby a very accurate sense of the country's geography. He enjoyed exchanging ideas with people from every social stratum, often living for long periods on the same rough food and in the same simple quarters as peasants and fishermen. These unusual practices were continued by Mongkut when, at the age of forty-seven, he finally ascended the throne of Thailand as Supreme Ruler and Lord of Life.

The twenty-seven years he had spent as a Buddhist monk, and later abbot, profoundly affected the monarch's subsequent behavior. Although he was a king-deity after a fashion unknown in the modern world (with the possible exception of the Japanese emperor, who was able to shed his heavy burden of sacred supremacy only after a prodigious military humiliation in 1946), Mongkut, on ascending the throne in 1851, embarked on reforms of a most progressive nature. With remarkable perspicacity, and an acute sense of historical inevitability, he accepted the fact that there was no way, even with the use of force, to keep Western nations out of Asia. He therefore decided to make them welcome. So great was his sense of urgency about what he recognized not only as the rise of a new kind of international diplomacy but as the emergence also of a new world-view, that he set out to learn English when well past his youth, hired the now-famous governess for his children and sent many of his young countrymen abroad to study. He insisted on equality under the law, set up printing presses, built roads and canals, created a modern currency, and was not too proud to ask French and English scientists and divines to exchange ideas with him and even "teach" him. In short, in his brief seventeen years as king he brought his medieval country to the status of a modern enlightened monarchy.

❖

It can be assumed that Mongkut's Buddhist training accounted for much of his exceptional behavior. In keeping with general Buddhist tolerance he showed a marked absence of religious bigotry, encouraging Western missionaries in their educational and medical work. When, however, he saw that certain Buddhist traditions were being threatened with destruction under the impact of Western influences, he did not look on passively. Instead, with the wisdom of a true philosopher who was also a man of action, he breathed new life into his country's form of Buddhism, thus helping to turn it into a vital force that unquestionably played a role in bringing Siam, with such surprising speed, out of its cocoon of insularity.

It is no part of this book's intention to weigh the relative merits, or the good and bad effects, of abandoning old ways of life and thought for new and alien ones. The real point is that Mongkut, singularly free of alleged Asian "fatalism," saw with his highly developed intuition how the tide of the times was running and decided to move with it; not, however, by simply allowing it to flow over him and his country but instead, in Buddhist fashion, by viewing this bit of world karma as "opportunity," and acting on it with his will and his wits.

The last great event of the king's life reveals the essential quality of the man. Among his many interests was astronomy, which he had learned from Western teachers. Scientific study of the heavens had become of such intense fascination for him that he was moved in 1868 to organize a tremendous private party in celebration of a solar eclipse, an event hitherto greeted in Siam by an ear-splitting din designed to scare off the demon who had the sun in his teeth and was attempting to swallow it!

Griswold's charming account of this eclipse-viewing event tells us a great deal about a monarch whose true nature was molded and modified by the highest Buddhist thought and practice of his time:

He calculated the exact moment when the total eclipse of 1868 would take place. Having determined that it could be seen best from a remote village in the southern part of his kingdom, near the east coast of the Malay Peninsula, he decided to give an intellectual house party there to observe it. He invited Sir Harry Ord, who had succeeded Butterworth as governor of Singapore, to sail up with a suite of officers and their ladies, and meet him at the appointed place. The French government would send a body of scientists from Paris. He himself would bring several of his wives and children, a number of government officials, and some Siamese gentlemen who were interested in astronomy. . . .

The royal party, sailing down the river and into the gulf, landed on the coast near the observation point. Workmen had been busy for months clearing a space in the forest beside the beach, building a great temporary palace and guest-house, and fitting up a special observatory. To the astonishment of most of the European guests—who were not yet acquainted with Siamese hospitality and had been looking forward with mixed emotions to the discomforts of a far-off jungle—the food was prepared by a French chef, the wines were served by an Italian *maître d'hôtel*, and the champagne was cooled with an abundance of ice, which was then the rarest of luxuries. In the evening, while companies of dancers performed episodes from the Indian epics, the King conversed informally with his guests. They had scarcely expected to see his ladies (don't Oriental monarchs always keep their wives locked up in a stuffy harem?)—yet there they were, neither timid nor aloof, but graceful and perfectly at ease. And nothing could have been more delightful than the royal children, with their pretty manners and their English chit-chat.

At dawn on the day of the eclipse there were dense clouds and a disappointing rain, but before the eclipse was over, the clouds had broken away and this great solar event could be viewed in all its awesome mystery. Although the people of the nearby villages had set about letting off firecrackers as was customary, the king remarked with utmost urbanity to his distinguished guests that they must not think these ignorant people were trying to frighten off a demon; they were merely "celebrating their sovereign's skill in having been able to calculate the moment of the eclipse more accurately than the European astronomers."

The story of the career of Mongkut, who as a ruler of Thailand did live like a king as well as a practicing Buddhist, illustrates the Hinayana teaching that there is only one way to be a Buddhist and that is to live by the precepts laid down by the Buddha over two thousand years ago. Although this is as true of Mahayana as of Theravada, it seems fair to state that the Theravada School, eschewing, in general, metaphysical flights and learned dialectic, has adhered more strictly to the form in which the Buddha cast his first sermon at Benares shortly after his Enlightenment.* In this Benares sermon, it will be remembered, the Buddha first set forth his conviction that until every being becomes truly enlightened a man cannot hope to escape dissatisfaction, since he shares the common human lot of all his fellows. Existence itself makes man subject not only to fleshly ills and eventual death but to all the frustrations and pain occasioned by the immutable laws of impermanence. It is the undeniable transience of all conditions which gives even joy its opposite face of sadness.

The criticism that this basic Buddhist doctrine of *dukkha* constitutes too pessimistic a view of life is countered with the statement that Buddhist concepts are actually no more pessimistic than such a familiar Christian description of the human world as "a vale of tears." In fact, Buddhism should be fairly called optimistic, since it avers the possibility of finding lasting peace in the midst of continuous flux and unhappiness.

The Buddha was, of course, not unaware that the ordinary man does not readily subscribe to the notion that his life is suffering. Man is, in fact, obviously prepared to resist just such uncompromising analysis by setting out in single-hearted pursuit of satisfaction as if it actually represented a *constant*. Yet, in the Buddha's view, it was this very belief in the attainment of lasting happiness, in conventional human terms, that was the true source of suffering. Man, by his unwillingness to accept what he interprets as life's failure to give him, without stint, whatever he desires, finds

---

* Note should be made in this context, however, that the Theravada School does have a higher teaching of its own. Known as the *Abhidhamma* (in Sanskrit, *Abhidharma*), it is a lengthy and complex commentary on, and analysis of, the Buddha's teaching and is closely related to *Satipatthana*, or Mind Control. In recent times Western students have become particularly interested in this third division of the Pali Canon, to which scholarly Burmese and Sinhalese Buddhists have long given special attention.

himself caught in an emotional trap of his own making. This trap is the product of his ego. It takes form from the self's insatiable appetites and delusions, its enormous blind unattainable desires, its never-satisfied craving or thirst, *tanha* or in Sanskrit *trishna*. It is *tanha* which leads the individual to place a tacit demand on life which life by its very nature cannot fulfil.

How then can a man find peace in the midst of continuous blind striving and impermanence? There is only one way, and that way must teach the development of compassionate detachment and discernment; an ever-deepening awareness of the interdependence and relationship of the individual with the cosmos. As for a definite path to the development of such awareness, with its resultant dynamic tranquillity, there is only one hope: *directed meditation or constant mindfulness*.

From the early years of his ministry the Buddha had recognized the necessity of devising a method by which the average man might be helped to escape his existential trap. This method was given specific form in the famous Eightfold Path, which if properly understood and conscientiously followed would, so it was asserted, lead to freedom from the universal bondage of ignorance and the spell of the personal ego.

The steps of this eightfold method, which leads to freedom, cannot be repeated too often since they constitute the basic psychological and therapeutic doctrine of the Buddha's Middle Way, passing between the two extremes of easy illusion and self-indulgence on the one hand and morbid asceticism or despair on the other. Enlightenment is attainable by adherence to a basic behavioral substructure built on right views, right thought or motivation, right speech, right action, right livelihood, right effort, right mindfulness and right concentration.

Although these eight steps of the Middle Way serve all Buddhists, they are particularly stressed in Theravada teaching, in which they are dwelt on and studied in precise analytical detail and with a special emphasis that constitutes not only a challenging *practice*, but effectively lifts them above the level of simple moral or ethical "recipes" and onto the plane of spiritual attainment.

Dr. H. Saddhatissa, the learned Theravada scholar, has written a book of admirable directness and clarity, *The Buddha's Way*, which cannot be recommended too highly for people anxious to understand original Buddhist precepts and the teaching of meditation as practiced in the Theravadin world.

In beginning his study of the way that leads to a balanced life, the author is careful to warn us that the truth of this ancient path to alleviation of suffering and the destruction of ignorance, although embodied in eight steps, is far from being a mere list to be studied and memorized. Each step, or "factor," as he terms it, must, rather, be vitally and dynamically assimilated into one's daily existence as constituting direct training for more acute states of consciousness. Moreover, one should not view the eight steps as having a consecutive development, but rather to understand them as interdependent and to be "simultaneously" perfected.

True to the psychological orientation of Buddhist teaching in general, it is suggested that before an aspirant begins specific practices leading to peace of mind and relief from tension he should undertake a certain amount of self-analysis, trying to ascertain, as far as possible, the existing state of his consciousness; for instance, what mental and emotional traits have already been developed to a certain extent and which remain truly rudimentary. One person may have a strongly developed thinking faculty and little if any ability to communicate with his fellow-men, while another might find it easy to establish feeling relationships with people yet have minimal reflective capacity. In other words, whatever one can know in advance about possible personal imbalances can help in the eventual development, under special discipline, of a well-rounded character.

It should be kept in mind that in Theravada Buddhism, although the path to liberation is grounded in the inescapable universal law of cause and effect—which is to say, all that we have been, thought, or done not only in this life but in other lives as well has affected our present circumstances—nonetheless each of us is in this very moment, whether consciously or *unconsciously*, *determining his future*. The importance of the "here and now," so emphasized in all Buddhist teaching, rises from the belief that the present offers the one opportunity in which the interrelated chain of cause and effect can, as it were, be *interrupted and transformed*.

The first of the Eight Steps to "release" is known to Theravadins as *samma ditthi*, which is to say, "right understanding" or "right views." The taking of this first step usually has its origin in a vague recognition that all is not well, things are out of joint, something is wrong—a general state of mind from which more and more modern people appear to be suffering. Fame, material security, success, power, do not seem to bring the peace and satisfaction that might be expected; further, there is a widespread uneasy feeling that no amount of confession or psychoanalytic catharsis quite wipes the slate clean or relieves anxiety about the consequences of past misdeeds or even of past *unconscious* mistakes. At this point of angst and malaise—if undergoing "insight meditation training"—one must strive to stop thinking automatically, to learn instead how to look at and to *see* things as they *really are*. Here one should strive to penetrate more deeply and personally into Buddha's teaching, not only on *dukkha* (things are obviously out of kilter) but on *anicca* (all things are impermanent). From this deepened realization of the significance of *dukkha* and *anicca* one should also glimpse the truth that conditions can be altered by a change of viewpoint—specifically, by the development of *anatta*, freedom from the tyranny of the ego.

Step Number Two, *samma sankappa*, which is usually translated as "right thought" or "right motive," applies, in Dr. Saddhatissa's words, "to the emotional basis of thought rather than to thinking itself." If Step One deals with the content and direction of thought, then Step Two is concerned with the kind and quality of "the drive behind the thinking." This invisible and often unrecognized emotional drive is considered of the utmost importance. With commendable directness the author of *The Buddha's Way* proceeds to point out how Buddha's original statements may be easily misinterpreted in modern times. For instance, those who are driven by the wish to avoid all unpleasant involvement in the manifold problems of contemporary life might speciously remind themselves of the Buddha's words that "everything is impermanent," so why bother? Or again, a pathological inability to relax and enjoy the wonder, pleasures and beauties of the world might easily lead to a false indifference based on the statement "all is suffering," a conclusion which might effectively shift the emphasis away from one's own personal insufficiency and put the blame, so to speak, on the cosmos, or "the way things are." Further, and very important, the Buddhist doctrine that there is nothing permanent or abiding, including the ego or a personal identity, might provide false reassurance for one who has never been able to form a satisfactory relationship with another human being, or for that matter even with himself.

The development of right thought in terms of the Buddha's Path means therefore a gradual uncovering and resolution of unrecognized interior drives, until at last a practitioner is able to observe that although he may *seem* to be thinking and acting with clarity and logic there is, in fact, an emotional block (perhaps more than one) controlling the direction of his so-called "reasoning" and preventing it from moving beyond a fixed familiar point. Therefore the mastering of the Second Step will be characterized by the disappearance of emotional obstructions as well as considerations of self-interest, and thus the elimination of those tensions and anxieties rooted in the ego and ego drives.

The Third Step, *samma vaca* or "right speech," has enormous contemporary significance. Dr. Saddhatissa tells us that we are following this ancient precept when we "use conversation as a means of coming to know people, to understand them and ourselves." How far contemporary humanity has moved from the idea of words as meaningful tools of exchange can, Dr. Saddhatissa suggests, be observed by anyone who sits quietly in a bus or train and listens to the talk around him. Almost without exception he will overhear merely a series of monologues with each participant in the so-called conversation interested only in what he has to say himself, paying little heed, in fact barely listening, to what his companions have to say. This behavior is very far removed from right speech. Disregard of this basic precept also accounts for the kind of mental and emotional fare offered the public today through newspapers, films, television, magazines, books, indeed all types of "communication" which not only develop but force-feed the growing appetite for violence, sensation and mindless escape.

Following right speech, among the Eight Steps, comes *samma kammanta*, or "right action," which signifies much more than merely abiding by such fundamental ethical principles as refraining from lying, stealing, overindulging in stimulants and so on. Although, to begin with, following such simple rules of conduct may not seem a very profound form of practice, it should eventually lead to a realization of this Fourth Precept's deep import. True *samma kammanta* or right action can arise only from "an unobstructed mind," a state of serenity which must begin with basic "wholesome" actions.

Here it is important to realize that, whereas in our Western religious tradition sins and virtues are matters of "Thou shalt" and "Thou shalt not," the Theravada Buddhist has no similar commandments. There are instead, counsels of perfection which begin "It is better to . . ." or "It is better not to . . ." follow such and such a course of action. This type of instruction leaves the choice of behavior to the individual, who remains free to verify through his own experience the wisdom of these suggestions.

With *samma ajiva*, Step Five, we come to the rather tricky point of "right livelihood." In the past, among Buddhists, this was a relatively uncomplicated matter, involving avoidance of butchering cattle, selling fish, hunting, warfare. Today the problems raised by the conscientious practice of this Fifth Step are subtle and intricate. Without attempting to give specific solutions, Dr. Saddhatissa presents some telling examples of the kind of predicament a practicing Buddhist may find himself facing in contemporary life.

1. Can one support "by working, paying taxes and accepting benefits, a government which is engaged in warfare, or actively preparing for it?"

2. Can one "in the name of the relief of human suffering, engage in medical research that involves sacrificing the lives of countless animals; and, more subtly, can one prescribe, sell—or even use—those drugs which have

been discovered and tested by means of such experiments?"

3. Has one the right to destroy possible "disease-bearing insects, or work in the preparation of materials for that purpose?"

4. Would "the third and fourth precepts prohibit one from working in advertising or mass production?"

In his widely read and influential classic, *Small Is Beautiful*, the noted British economist E. F. Schumacher (who was, incidentally, a devout Roman Catholic) has an arresting chapter on "Buddhist economics." He points out that Buddhist economics in its essence (and regardless of whether practiced today in Buddhist countries or not) differs radically from the prevailing economics of modern materialism. He describes how Buddhism, in the light of the precept of Right Livelihood, sees daily work as a means for the purification of human character. Only through healthily employed individuals, able to find integrity, concentration and equanimity in their work-life, does the optimum situation for the development of a strong and compassionate society exist.

Dealing with the pressing problems of ecology and the environment in today's culture, Schumacher quotes tellingly from Bertrand de Jouvenel, the French political philosopher whose description of Western man seems to him a fair characterization of the average modern economist. "He tends to count nothing as an expenditure, other than human effort; he does not seem to mind how much mineral matter he wastes and, far worse, how much living matter he destroys."

This form of myopia, in such marked contrast to Buddhist teaching, is, it is hoped, beginning to disappear under the stress of present-day economic realities. Even though people in some Buddhist countries, in their current pursuit of "progress" Western style, may appear to care little for their ancient spiritual heritage, it cannot be denied that the Buddhist stress on the interrelatedness of all life and the necessity of developing nonviolent and nondestructive attitudes—from the point of view of mere survival, if nothing more—has an ever-sharper pertinence on the contemporary scene. Schumacher, it should be noted, was writing his chapter on Buddhist economics in 1973. A warm, tough-minded and, above all, practical economist, he saw then that the people depending on a high-use rate of nonrenewable natural resources were, in effect, "performing an act of violence against nature" which must almost inevitably lead to "violence between men." The way out in his view did not involve a drastic choice between "growth and stagnation," but rather the finding of a "right path of development," a "middle way between materialistic heedlessness and immobility," in short, a new-old way of practicing the laws of "right livelihood."

The road to right livelihood is not easy. It demands careful evaluation of many factors and circumstances. In order to handle life with dynamism and conscientiousness, it may be necessary to "take time out" for a deeply thoughtful consideration as to how we are going to spend the precious hours of our work-life. From the point of view of a Theravadin, Dr. Saddhatissa in *The Buddha's Way* concludes his remarks on this subject with the words: "If a job helps us in our search for an understanding both of ourselves and of the world around us then it is, for us, *samma ajiva* (right livelihood)—no matter how futile and crazy it may seem to our friends and neighbors."

*Samma vayama* or "right effort" (Number Six) can be divided into four categories of practice:

1. The effort to cut off unwholesome states that have already arisen

2. The effort to prevent the arising of unwholesome states that have not yet arisen

3. The effort to preserve the wholesome states that have already arisen

4. The effort to encourage wholesome states that have not yet arisen

Even from the most cursory study of this deliberately simplified list, we can see that the development of insight, intuition and will power are all plainly a part of the Sixth Step. Insight gives clear perception of one's existing state of mind; intuition (developed through meditation and mindfulness) allows that insight to work in such a way that we see our mind's direction; will power is the inner strength by which we can alter the habitual patterns of our thought processes and thus effect changes in our character.

Number Seven, *samma sati*, or "right mindfulness," is the "pivotal factor of the path." The author refers us to the Christian phrase "the practice of the presence of God" as being comparable to that state of consciousness which finally makes possible "full awareness" applied to every thought, word and deed.

Mindfulness of the body is a part of *samma sati*, an awareness which might begin with the sort of exercise undertaken by Admiral Shattock in the Burmese monastery mentioned earlier, and so clearly described in his book *An Experiment in Mindfulness*. This valuable record of a Westerner's experience in certain meditative methods of Theravada Buddhism* tells us how the admiral, who had gone for training to a monastery near Rangoon, was given only two basic exercises to do, but he did them all day, alternately. One was to walk back and forth a specified short distance for a given period of time with his consciousness totally fixed on the separate actions involved in taking a step: "up, forward, down." The object was to "break the apparent continuity of the mind." This seemingly simple but actually difficult exercise—along with the second one, which required concentrated awareness of the gentle rise and fall of the abdomen in breathing—served, in a few weeks, to make very clear to the admiral the essentially undisciplined nature of his highly "trained" mind. He was, he discovered, at the mercy of innumerable, intrusive, apparently uncontrollable, darting and fluttering "butterfly thoughts."

At the end of Shattock's relatively brief period as a Theravadin novice, he had come to several surprising personal conclusions, among them that much of Western education and "mind-training" methods seemed to him like the stuffing of geese to produce *pâté de foie gras* in contrast to Buddhist methods which, in his experi-

* See also *A Meditator's Diary*, Jane Hamilton-Merritt, New York, Harper and Row, 1976.

ence, began the process of education by training the mind to allow "*access to insight.*"

Even in a few weeks of practicing Insight Meditation (*Satipatthana*) daily, Admiral Shattock found himself experiencing an unfamiliar bodily awareness, a new and more steady state of physical and mental control. The training he was undergoing was not designed to involve the mind in endless scrutiny or analysis of specific bodily action; its purpose was rather to "eliminate the bondage of unreflective habituation through the development of a total alert awareness." This "noting-without-attachment" to any mental or physical event is aimed at easing tensions on even an unconscious level.

Special attention is placed in these exercises on breathing awareness or respiration mindfulness, since the simple but sustained exercise of observing one's breath is capable of carrying the faithful practitioner beyond the state of *attachment* not only to his physical being but to his illusory ego as well.

We will have occasion to refer to breath training a number of times in this section on practice and teaching, for all types of Buddhist meditation make use of basic exercises in respiration mindfulness. In the words of one teacher of Insight Meditation, "the incoming and outgoing of the breath accompanied by the rise and fall of the abdomen vividly illustrate the transient and fluctuating nature of the bodily organism. The activities of the body come into being and pass away time and again. There is obviously nothing inherently permanent about the physical body. Not only is there ongoing aging eventuating in death, each moment of conscious life is an ebb and flow process as seen in the rise and fall of the breath." Words like these cause one to reflect on the probable influence of such teaching on the Buddhist attitude toward dying; an attitude which seems in its calm positiveness and serene acceptance to differ so markedly from Western reactions to life's inevitable end.

The term for mindfulness of the body is *samma sati*, and final attainment of this condition might also begin with physical disciplines not unlike those Admiral Shattock undertook in Burma. There are a number of possible approaches, but whatever the initial mode of instruction the aim is the same: the acquiring of a state of consciousness in relation to one's physical being which is simultaneously objective and subjective. The line drawn is subtle but definite. We are not to look at our bodies as mere "things" moving like puppets before the observing mind, nor are we to feel with too acute a personal perception every single movement and gesture. What we are aiming at is the unstrained ability to live here and now in our bodies, a condition almost never experienced without special training. (In the modern West, types of instruction similar to those given by Charlotte Selver and Charles Brooks in their courses in Sensory Awareness and by other experimenters in the sensory field are moving toward a kind of bodily awareness new to our part of the world.)*

Dr. Saddhatissa describes the various ways by which mindfulness of the body can be practiced: by watching the breath flowing in and out of the nostrils, by consciously listening to the sounds that strike our ear, without pausing to name and pass judgment on them but just noting their arising and passing away, even by becoming aware of the taste and texture of food, not in the manner of a gourmet nor with the wish to become an expert on taste experiences but merely to intensify every aspect of daily awareness.

Along with the development of bodily mindfulness comes also the mindfulness of one's feelings and even the mindfulness of one's mind. As for our feelings, we should neither develop a cold mechanistic response to them nor cling to them; rather we should *quietly watch their arising and passing away as also with each thought*, until gradually identification with our feelings and thoughts disappears and this, quite "naturally," without making any use of what we in the West would call suppression, repression or even expression.

The Eight Steps of the Theravada path culminate in *samma samadhi*, usually translated as "right concentration" or "right meditation," although its real meaning is complete unification in which subject and object become one. Here it is suggested that it would be a mistake to equate this kind of meditation with what the

* *Sensory Awareness: The Rediscovery of Experiencing*, Charles V. W. Brooks, An Esalen Book, The Viking Press, Inc., New York, 1974.

Christian also terms meditation. "Contemplation" might be nearer the mark. It is generally agreed that there is no adequate translation for this culminating stage. It could be said that in *samma samadhi*, in a sense, the practitioner moves from observation to nonobservation to participation and finally into absorption, as in the metaphor used earlier of the ocean entering the drop.

In a general book of limited scope it is plainly not possible to consider even in brief detail all the varieties of Theravada meditation. Certain "character-correcting" exercises have been helpfully compressed into a basic four which may be, and often are, practiced each day for a period even as brief as twenty minutes if the circumstances of an individual's life make it necessary to allot only limited segments of time for meditation.

The first of these familiar exercises for Buddhists following the Theravada path comprises a devotional meditation on the Buddha, his Teaching, and the *Sangha*. Often called Recollection of the Triple Gem, it stresses, to begin with, thoughtful contemplation of the qualities exemplified by the Great Teacher who was—and this is of special significance in the Theravada tradition—*born a man*. Realization that the Buddha was not supernatural or divine should, it is held, strengthen one's faith in personal effort and intensify the belief that the goal of heightened consciousness *can* be reached. Second, in meditation on the Teaching itself, the meditator should find further support for his own endeavors. Third, out of his own personal experiences, there should arise ever more sincere feelings of gratitude for the brotherhood of other believers, past and present, and a strong desire to help all others live out the Buddha's precepts in daily life.

From this Triple Gem meditation on the Buddha, the Teaching, and the *Sangha*, the individual moves to a meditation on his own body. First focusing his mind on his skin, he begins with the upper lip, traveling across his face to pass over the top and the back of his head, then down to his feet and up the front again as far as the lower lip. From the skin surface, following the same progression, he next focuses his awareness on the flesh beneath the skin, and third, on the skeletal structure; the bones. He then reverses the order; bones, flesh, skin.

It is to be understood that this is not an exercise in reviewing one's knowledge of anatomy; it is designed rather to heighten awareness of the body and by stimulating "analytical faculties" bring about a lessening of attachment to the total physical self, not, however, with any sense of repudiation of the physical in favor of the spiritual. In general in Buddhist teaching, emphasis is placed on the Buddha's injunction that eventual fulfillment is not to be found while rigidly denying the body's needs—its "reality," one might say—but while living the life of the ordinary human being. It will be recalled that one of Gautama's great breakthroughs prior to his Enlightenment came with the realization that the body is the essential vehicle of salvation. An abused or denied corpus can hardly be of help in any endeavor to solve life's meaning. It was at this point in his progressive personal illumination that the Buddha, abandoning his long-held traditional ascetic's pose, rose to bathe in the nearby river and afterward walked to the nearest village to beg alms for his wasted body.

This change of attitude on the Buddha's part merits the most careful attention by all students of Buddhism's tenets. When the Buddha came to realize that he was effectively distracting himself from his deepest intention by denying his body the care it needed, he took the first notable step away from the ego's singular "body-mind identification." Later, after his Enlightenment, we find him seeking to free his disciples of this same unconscious identification. This he did by designating specific exercises to aid in ridding them of their mistaken perception of the personal ego, the narcissistic attachment to their individual physical beings. He suggested visiting graveyards and charnel grounds. He also prescribed the listing and memorizing of the body's parts and functions. Some of these exercises may strike us today as rather unpleasantly graphic, particularly those that name the body's "manifold impurities," but they were not prescribed with the intention of casting a shadow on all physical processes. Their aim, rather, was to place proper emphasis on the body as not only a transitory *instrument* inseparable from the mind but also as the means, because of this very mind-body inseparability, of bringing about man's eventual release from a crippling delusion. Buddha's sense of the importance of corporeal being is expressed in the well-known scriptural passage: "Within this very body, mortal as it is and only six feet in length, I do declare to you are the world and the origin of the world, and the ceasing of the world, and likewise the Path that leads to the cessation thereof."

The meditator who has, as described in the preceding paragraphs, been striving to heighten awareness of his body through its skin, flesh and bones should now find it quite natural to move on to a consideration of this very body's inevitable dissolution. Meditation on death is, therefore, a logical sequence in these particular Theravada Buddhist exercises. By contrast with the general Western suppression or evasion of the inescapable fact of death, so common in modern times, Buddhism places a quiet, taken-for-granted emphasis on life's end. This is done in the hope of stimulating energy and a sense of urgency about "getting on with it" in the immediate Now; it is also seen as training for the inevitable moment when the time does come to leave the world.

In the Buddhist view, meditation on death is not considered in the least morbid. It is believed to serve mental health by keeping life's "wholeness" in balance. Reminding us of the immutable law of change and impermanence that rests at life's core, it should help to eradicate feelings of greed and possessiveness, of "me" and "mine." More than this, it should increase man's gratitude for the rare opportunity given him in attaining a human body with all its marvelous equipment to work with and through—a happening never to be lightly or thoughtlessly taken for granted. The pervasive emphasis on eternal youth, so common a part of contemporary culture, seems to many Buddhists to indicate a dangerous imbalance. Dr. Saddhatissa, too, reminds us that this imbalance was not always present in the Western world. In the Middle Ages, for instance, by an act of "simple sanity" a skull was often placed in the center of the table at a feast. Earlier, in Roman days, a victorious general walking in triumph through the streets among the cheers and plaudits of the populace was ritualistically accompanied by a man who whispered to him as he walked, "Remember you are only mortal." And later, to be sure, the Christian Church emphasized (and not always with gloom) the necessity of contemplating one's own death.

Following the Theravada meditation on the Triple Gem, moving from there to the body and the body's demise, we come fourthly to *metta*, a singularly vital practice in the giving forth of universal love. *Metta* is not an exercise in charity or in sentimental good will; it does not deal in fuzzy abstractions. A directed dynamic suffusion of one's whole being with active love and benevolence, it entails not only the deliberate creation of such a state of being but the power to send forth, from one's innermost center, unfailing compassion, concern and loving-kindness.

Some years ago I attended a Buddhist seminar in Roehampton, England. Many eminent Buddhists, including I. B. Horner, the great Pali scholar, and Dr. Edward Conze, were present, along with a miscellany of middle-aged followers of the Buddha's way and young people just tentatively beginning to study and experiment. Our instructor in the morning meditation was a revered *thera**\* from Colombo whom I had met not long before on a trip to Sri Lanka. This noted teacher had come to London from his beautiful tropical island to help establish a Buddhist practice center, in a cold, noisy, damp and—at that time—very polluted city.

The subject this gentle little sage gave us for our early morning meditation was *metta*. His instructions were direct and specific. To begin with, we were to extend love to ourselves, since if we could not love ourselves we surely could not love anyone else. From ourselves we were to move our feelings of good will and benevolence outward, including all those in the room with us, to distant relatives and friends (not, however, with any sentimentality or possessiveness); moving ever out and out, *without losing concentration*, we were to include all those less well known or who "meant nothing

\* *Thera:* an honorary title in Theravada Buddhism—a senior member of the *Sangha*, an Elder of exceptional character.

to us," to total strangers, and finally to our enemies. We were, in short, asked to suffuse our entire beings with the dynamic force of *metta* and project it outward from our own centers until it embraced the whole universe. There was nothing simple, simple-minded or abstract about this demanding daily exercise. Under our instructor's quiet tutelage I believe most of us became aware of *metta*'s inherent dynamism and power.

Some members of the class, however, raised an objection to this daily exercise. Word of dissatisfaction with *metta* as a meditation subject reached the *thera* and so, at the beginning of one morning's session, he rose to inquire about the accuracy of this reported dissent. After a rather awkward pause a young woman stood up and said, somewhat defensively, that as Christians almost everyone present had been brought up on the tenet of brotherly love; it was indeed, even if generally unpracticed, a very familiar concept in Christian theology. Some of the class thought, therefore, that an exercise in "getting rid of the ego"—a point which was not stressed in Christianity as strongly as in Buddhism—might prove more useful.

The *thera* appeared sincerely interested in this view. He asked if others shared the feeling just expressed. A few raised their hands; some nodded assent. The *thera* expressed his gratitude for the suggestion and promised to give it careful consideration. For that morning, however, he proposed we all continue to work on the dynamic practice of *metta*.

In the remaining days of the seminar the morning meditation was not changed; nor was the matter of dissatisfaction over the subject ever referred to again publicly. By the end of the period it must have been clear to any thoughtful person that if one could learn how really to practice *metta*, problems with the ego would begin to disappear. This particular Buddhist exercise is designed to teach the practitioner not to separate himself from the rest of humanity, even though he has deliberately embarked on the "task of *self*-liberation."

Before leaving the all-important Theravada Buddhist teaching of *metta*, it might be well to insert here the actual words of this beautiful injunction to universal compassion and love.

May all beings be happy and at their ease. May they be joyous and live in safety! All beings, whether weak or strong—omitting none—in high, middle or low realms of existence, small or great, visible or invisible, near or far away, born or to be born—may all beings be happy and at their ease! Let none deceive another, or despise any being in any state; let none by anger or ill-will wish harm to another! Even as a mother watches over and protects her child, her only child, so with boundless mind should one cherish all living beings, radiating friendliness over the entire world, above, below and all around without limits; so let him cultivate a boundless goodwill towards the entire world, uncramped, free from ill-will or enmity.

The four kinds of Theravada meditation described just above—(1) recollection of the Triple Gem: the Buddha, the Teaching, the *Sangha*; (2) meditation on the body; (3) meditation on the body's demise; (4) *metta*—may be taken to represent types of practice to be embarked on when the meditator, for whatever reason, is not able to spend such concentrated periods of time as those required of one who sets out to work formally in either of the two chief categories of Theravada meditation: *samatha* and *vipassana*.

We will now briefly consider these two vitally significant Theravada meditation exercises which together may be said to comprise *Satipatthana*, the practice of full mindfulness, also expressed as "awareness of attentiveness."

*Samatha* is defined as the development of calm and concentration.

*Vipassana* is the development of *insight*, which would seem to require stricter procedures, since it involves more than the mere attainment of calmness and serenity.

Certain *samatha* practices are designed as specific aids in the focusing and quieting of the mind. One of these aids is the use of a colored disc or *kasina*, constructed by the meditator himself, placed in a suitable spot and then concentrated on—without, however, staring or straining. This fixing on a visible object is to be followed by closing the eyes and visualizing the disc in memory.

There is another *samatha* meditation exercise which involves the repetition of a special word or sequence of words. This practice reminds one of the type of training so widely given at present in

Transcendental Meditation and of the "prayer of the heart," the Jesus Prayer, as used by monks of the Greek Orthodox faith. It is of course also related to the utterance of sacred syllables or mantra in other Buddhist branches as well as in Hinduism.

Perhaps the most frequently used exercise in *samatha* meditation is that referred to before as "the recollection of in-breathing and out-breathing" for which the Theravada term is *anapanasati*. Breathing exercises are common, as already noted, to all Buddhist traditions, since breath control was one of the methods of mind-stilling employed by the Buddha at the time of his Enlightenment. In *samatha* breathing, it is suggested that the meditator focus his attention on the tip of the nostrils and, without squinting, hold his consciousness steady at this point to "watch the breath as it flows in and out. He may count the breaths or not as wished. His basic concern is how best to *anchor* his *concentration*."

It is impossible to elaborate on the many significant benefits said to arise from *samatha* meditation. The various devices—the use of the *kasina*, the recitation of sacred syllables, breath mindfulness —are all designed (along with others, not mentioned here) to serve as aids in quieting the mind's restless undisciplined activity. Stilling the mind is seen as the only means to tranquillity and balanced behavior. Side effects like ecstatic trances or the ability to perform "miracles" may come as a result of advanced *samatha* practice, but they are to be minimized; achievements of this kind are not the correct goal of meditation practice. The Buddha warned specifically and strongly against the cultivation or public display of any special or supernatural powers. In this respect he is sometimes compared to Christ in his rejection of Satan's invitation or "temptation" to demonstrate his divinity by casting himself from a high place without sustaining injury. In Buddhism, faith in the performance of miracles, even the ability to perform them (a freely admitted possibility), is in no way as important as discovery of the inner truths of one's own nature on the slower path of daily personal endeavor.

*Vipassana*—the second of the two practices that comprise *Satipatthana*—is considered the highest meditation form in Theravada. Its goal is the development not alone of tranquillity but of true insight, the ability to see things as they really are in all their "suchness." *Vipassana* employs methods similar to those used in *samatha* but with a significantly different purpose. Whereas in *samatha* the basic aim is to quiet the restless mind, to induce a calmer state of being and a more serene response to life, in *vipassana* the mind, after becoming calm and focused, is then led on, even "goaded," to look carefully into the appearance of things, and, in a sense, *behind* these appearances. In *vipassana* breathing exercises the meditator, instead of being trained to center his attention on the tip of his nostrils past which he feels his breath flowing in and out, is asked to observe the physical phenomena of the moving breath itself: the relative character of in-breath, out-breath, pause, in-breath again. In *samatha*, any disturbances including personal reactions that arise during meditation are to be avoided if possible, and ignored if they do occur. On the contrary, in *vipassana*, the meditator is particularly to *notice* his reactions, as for instance, "thinking," "feeling," "hurting," "desiring" and so on.

During a college course in Buddhist instruction given at Oberlin in 1969, some helpful clues to *vipassana* meditation were offered to the students by the Venerable Dhammasudhi, a noted Theravadin Teacher:

The only requirement on the practical side is for you to give full attention to the sensory processes. When your full attention is given to hearing—not only the sound heard but also the subject who is hearing with all the conditions and states of that subject—several consequences follow. . . . understanding based on truly objective analytical knowledge is one result. Moreover, when you give full attention to the senses, they become tranquil because there is no distraction or selective exclusion. . . .

When you hear, or see, or touch, there is a strong feeling of, "*I am* hearing, *I am* seeing, *I am* touching." At that particular moment it is very important for you to be aware of the "I am," how "I am" operates— *not to be "I am" but to be aware of "I am."* This is meditation. When you *become* "I am," you identify yourself with the "I," and then you have no power to see or understand because self-control or controlling power has been lost. When "I am" becomes too powerful, it instils in you a sense of agent so that you become interpreter, creator, liker, etc. . . .

Dr. Dhammasudhi went on to explain that by becoming truly aware of the "I" as it operates and reacts, one will begin to gain real controlling power over seeing, hearing, touching, tasting, smelling, even thinking. Only through the growth of such detached awareness can one hope to become in time free of that blinding "self-identification" which prevents our ever seeing things *as they really are*. He pointed out how in this process of sensory awareness one can find no proof of any basic individual "self" who sees or hears. Apart from awareness of seeing, hearing, feeling, thinking and so on, there exists no self-entity—which brings us back to the Western philosopher quoted earlier, David Hume, who reported on the failure of his attempt to find any true "self" separate from physical "conditions."

The assiduous practice of *vipassana*, it is claimed, will therefore help the individual meditator overcome existential torment, supplanting it with a sense of ease and well-being; a state which naturally and inevitably arises from the gradual disappearance of the isolating sense of "I," the personal ego, with all its attendant and related illusions and demands.

It should be repeated that the state of desirelessness which accompanies "insight" is by no means to be understood as indifference, nor is it related to that familiar contemporary attitude of rejection of the world's seemingly insoluble problems out of personal despair. Once again, one is reminded, the Buddha's teaching emphasizes that "liberation" is to be sought not apart from, but in the very midst of the confusion, controversy, paradox, strivings, failure and general existential suffering which characterize and unite all life. As a modern Theravadin has remarked wryly, we must "somehow work out our salvation in the midst of the nuclear arms race and surrounded by our bingo-crazy relations."

If followers of the Theravada way often give the appearance of a special gentleness and benevolence, this is no indication of any undue softness at the core of the teaching. The effort involved in becoming truly concentrated and disciplined is indeed so strenuous that we find it expressed in an early Pali scripture, the Anguttaranikaya, in terms of warfare itself. In an exchange between the Great Teacher and his disciples, we read lines which remind us of Christ's often sadly misinterpreted words, "I come not to bring peace but a sword."

> "Warriors, warriors, Lord, we call ourselves.
>   In what way are we warriors?"
> "We wage war, Brethren; therefore are we
>   called warriors."
> "Wherefore, Lord, do we wage war?"
> "For lofty virtue, for high endeavor, for
>   sublime wisdom—for these things do we
>   wage war. Therefore we are called warriors."

In conclusion, there could be no clearer summation of the general attitude of the loving but strict Theravada than that offered by the noted Burmese *bhikkhu* U Thittila, in three paragraphs of "The Fundamental Principles of Theravada Buddhism," contributed by him to Kenneth Morgan's anthology *The Path of the Buddha.*

All the teachings of the Buddha can be summed up in one word: Dhamma. The Sanskrit form of the word is *Dharma*, but in the Pali language . . . it is softened to Dhamma. It means truth, that which really is. It also means law, the law which exists in a man's own heart and mind. It is the principle of righteousness. Therefore the Buddha appeals to man to be noble, pure, and charitable not in order to please any Supreme Being, but in order to be true to the highest in himself.

Dhamma, this law of righteousness, exists not only in a man's heart and mind, it exists in the universe also. All the universe is an embodiment and revelation of Dhamma. When the moon rises and sets, the rains come, the crops grow, the seasons change, it is because of Dhamma, for Dhamma is the law residing in the universe which makes matter act in the ways revealed by the studies of modern science in physics, chemistry, zoology, botany, and astronomy. Dhamma is the true nature of every existing thing, animate and inanimate.

If a man will live by Dhamma, he will escape misery and come to Nibbana, the final release from all suffering. It is not by any kind of prayer, nor by any ceremonies, nor by any appeal to a deity or a God that a man will discover the Dhamma which will lead him to his goal. He will discover it in only one way—by developing his own character. This development comes only through control of the mind and purification of the emotions. Until a man stills the storm in his heart, until he extends his loving-kindness to all beings, he will not be able to take even the first step toward his goal.

A true perception of the strong Hinayana emphasis on the Buddha as an Enlightened Man, not a Divine Savior, comes to many Westerners on viewing the ancient stone statues of Sri Lanka. Particularly impressive among these figures are the ones still to be seen in the ancient ruined city of Polonnaruwa, the capital of Sinhalese Buddhist kings from the eighth to the twelfth century. In these ruins of a lost Golden Age there survive three colossal figures of Buddha carved from enormous stones. One Buddha is seated in meditation before a cave entrance; in the cave itself is another seated figure and outside the cave, reclining in an open green space, is the Buddha in his hour of death (*Parinirvana*) with his devoted disciple Ananda standing beside him.

No Westerner has described more intimately than Thomas Merton the powerful effect on him of these ancient Buddha figures, in particular that of the dying Buddha. In the *Asian Journal* on which this Trappist monk and scholar was working at the time of his death in 1973, he wrote:

. . . I am able to approach the Buddhas barefoot and undisturbed, my feet in wet grass, wet sand. Then the silence of the extraordinary faces. The great smiles. Huge and yet subtle. Filled with every possi-

*Great Demise of the Buddha* (Parinirvana). *Gigantic reclining figure, lying in a quiet open countryside in Sri Lanka, with favorite disciple Ananda standing at his head. Twelfth century.*

*Buddha depicted in almost totally human terms, the hands in* mudra *of "inward absorption." Typical Theravadan conception of the Buddha as a supremely fulfilled man.*

bility, questioning nothing, knowing everything, rejecting nothing, the peace not of emotional resignation but of Madhyamika,* of sunyata,† that has seen through every question without trying to discredit anyone or anything—*without refutation*—*without establishing some other argument* [italics added]. For the doctrinaire, the mind that needs well-established positions, such peace, such silence, can be frightening. I was knocked over with a rush of relief and thankfulness at the *obvious* clarity of the figures, the clarity and fluidity of shape and line, the design of the monumental bodies composed into the rock shape and landscape, figure, rock and tree. And the sweep of bare rock sloping away on the other side of the hollow, where you can go back and see different aspects of the figures.

Looking at these figures I was suddenly, almost forcibly, jerked clean out of the habitual, half-tired vision of things, and an inner clearness, clarity, as if exploding from the rocks themselves, became evident and obvious. The queer *evidence* of the reclining figure [in the *Parinirvana*], the smile, the sad smile of Ananda standing with arms folded (much more "imperative" than Da Vinci's Mona Lisa because completely simple and straightforward). The thing about all this is that there is no puzzle, no problem, and really no "mystery." All problems are resolved and everything is clear, simply because what matters is clear. The rock, all matter, all life, is charged with dharmakaya‡ . . . everything is emptiness and everything is compassion. I don't know when in my life I have ever had such a sense of beauty and spiritual validity running together in one aesthetic illumination. . . .

Buddhist statues, when studied in detail or at close range, often give the onlooker a strong sense of livingness, a feeling that the figure at which he gazes is actually breathing with ·a controlled inner breath. It is impossible not to believe that the nameless artists

* *Madhyamika:* The Middle Way.
† *Sunyata:* Emptiness. Used in the sense of the absence of conception; better rendered as the plenum void: the infinite potentiality of existence.
‡ *Dharmakaya:* The Buddha Truth—consciousness merged in the universal consciousness.

*In certain ancient parts of today's Thailand, figures of the wandering Buddha as teacher became for a time popular icons. They were known as "Walking Buddhas." Bronze. School of Sukhodaya. Fourteenth century.*

who created these sublime images knew from their own personal experience about this inner breath. They too must have practiced meditative disciplines and have come themselves to understand the silence of "the great within."

P. D. Ouspensky—the Russian philosopher, who astounded the intellectual world in the 1920s and 1930s with his books *Tertium Organum* and *A New Model of the Universe*—has described in the latter a visit he made to see the famous statue of "the Buddha with Sapphire Eyes" in the country then called Ceylon. This Buddha was not openly displayed like those Merton saw; in fact Ouspensky had to be quite persistent before he was finally admitted to the monastery where the image was housed. What Ouspensky wrote in memory of this encounter effectively describes the sense of an actual living

presence which the greatest Buddhist figures—if studied in solitary silence, and with an openness of spirit—so tellingly convey.

The face of the Buddha was quite calm, but not expressionless, and full of deep thought and feeling. He was lying here deep in thought, and I had come, opened the doors and stood before him, and now he was involuntarily judging me. But there was no blame or reproach in his glance. His look was extraordinarily serious, calm and full of understanding. But when I attempted to ask myself what the face of the Buddha expressed, I realised that there could be no answer. His face was neither cold nor indifferent. On the other hand it would be quite wrong to say that it expressed warmth, sympathy or compassion. All this would be too small to ascribe to him. At the same time it would also be wrong to say that the face of the Buddha expressed unearthly grandeur or divine wisdom. No, it was a human face, yet at the same time a face which men do not happen to have. I felt that all the words I could command would be wrong if applied to the expression of this face. I can only say that here was *understanding*.

Simultaneously I began to feel the strange effect which the Buddha's face produced on me. All the gloom that rose from the depths of my soul seemed to clear up. It was as if the Buddha's face communicated its calm to me. Everything that up to now had troubled me and appeared so serious and important, now became so small, insignificant and unworthy of notice, that I only wondered how it could ever have affected me. And I felt that no matter how agitated, troubled, irritated and torn with contradictory thoughts and feelings a man might be when he came here, he would go away calm, quiet, enlightened, *understanding*. . . . I do not know of any work in Christian art which stands on the same level as the Buddha with the Sapphire Eyes, that is to say, I know of no work which expresses in itself so completely the idea of Christianity as the face of this Buddha expresses the idea of Buddhism. To understand this face is to understand Buddhism."

It seems self-evident that the anonymous artists who could express, with such compelling realism, qualities of utter peace and awareness must themselves have experienced what they were able so sublimely to portray, not in gods or saints, but in the faces and bodies of other human beings.

# Tibetan
# Buddhism

We have seen in the preceding chapter how the Hinayana of Southeastern Asia—Sri Lanka, Burma, Thailand—remained relatively true to the early or primitive teachings of the Buddha, abiding by the original basic tenet that each seeker must work out his own salvation by his own efforts. We have also seen how this original emphasis underwent certain inevitable changes as Buddhism, flowing with the tides of commerce, partly by sea and partly by land, made its way over the vast and varied Asian world. During its quiet, characteristically tolerant missionary journeying, Buddhism inevitably became a more catholic, less ascetic religion. In its various Mahayana forms there developed in time an inner core of esoteric doctrine including a pantheon of deities both benevolent and fearsome and a "lineage" of other Buddhas from the past, prior to Shakyamuni Buddha,* and in the future as well.

Many forms of Mahayana seem a far cry from early Hinayana's emphasis on the Buddha who was born and remained a man—albeit an enlightened man. It was not so much that Mahayana set out to reject Theravada teachings; it simply moved on in new directions as they presented themselves, geographically, culturally, his-

* One of the historic Buddha's many designations. It means the Sage (*Muni*) of the Shakyas, Siddhartha Gautama's family clan name.

torically. These encounters and expansions led to a quickened vitality in mythmaking, along with a tendency to psychological experimentation, metaphysical speculation and phantasmagoric art. These particular aspects of the Mahayana reached their most extreme and diversified expression when Buddhism in the seventh century A.D. entered the remote land of Tibet under a "tantric guise," strongly influenced by the mystical Indian cult of Shiva and his feminine energy, or *shakti*,\* a form of worship then prevalent in the neighboring Indian kingdom of Bengal.

For many centuries, Tibetan Buddhist teachings were hidden from the West behind a heavy veil of mystery, remoteness and misunderstanding. Not only was the land of Tibet almost impossible to visit, but its many wise men and great teachers were virtually inaccessible to all but a handful of the most ardent and intrepid adventurers. Among those very few valorous Western travelers of recent times who managed to get into this forbidden country and return to write books about it, certain names stand out: first of all, surely, the dauntless Frenchwoman Alexandra David-Neel, who in spite of seemingly insurmountable handicaps managed to penetrate Tibet's interior disguised as a lama and to emerge safely in due course with revelations of many esoteric teachings; then Marco Pallis, British-born, of Greek descent, a mountain climber, mystic and musician whose *Peaks and Lamas* is a classic study of inner as well as outer exploration; Giuseppe Tucci, the distinguished anthropologist and scholar; Fosco Maraini, the brilliant journalist-photographer; Heinrich Harrer, the Austrian prisoner of war who, during World War II, escaped from India into Tibet and lived there for seven years; and scholars like David Snellgrove, Hugh Richardson and a number of other informed impartial observers whose names are given in the bibliography.

It is not possible, or for that matter necessary, to delve into the complex network of reasons which account for Tibet's sustained rebuff of the Western world. In reading of this fabulous and beautiful land—so high and so remote, lying at the heart of the world's largest continent—and even in visiting neighboring countries like

\* In Tibet, the term *prajna* is used, not *shakti*.

Sikkim, Nepal and Bhutan, one is almost tempted to settle for the explanation, sometimes guardedly advanced, that there was a "cosmic plan" to keep Tibet's esoterica hidden from the merely curious or possibly vulgar exploiters until just the right moment in history. When China's reassertion in 1959 of its ancient suzerainty over Tibet created the danger of an immemorial body of religious wisdom vanishing forever from the earth, the necessity seems to have been accepted among many Tibetan masters that the time had come to share with the world at large their wealth of spiritual findings and practices.

The value of Tibet's contribution to Buddhism and, in fact, to man's spiritual and psychological history as a whole can hardly be overestimated. Because of its long isolation from the Western world, plus the formidable barrier created by its difficult language, Tibet has been able to maintain a vast and valuable storehouse of philosophical, psychological, metaphysical and even magical treasures dating from mankind's distant past.

Under the title of Tantrayana or Vajrayana, one can find in Tibetan Buddhism variants in teaching and practice ranging from the most conservative and balanced Theravada to the loftiest and most abstract flights of the Mahayana. Tibetan Buddhism also accommodates not only still-vital fragments of the native folk religion, a type of shamanism known as Bön, but in its wide range there coexist a down-to-earth pragmatism characteristic also of Zen, along with devotional worship comparable to Hindu *bhakti* or to that of the Pure Land Sect of Japan, already mentioned.

The power and influence of the several great Tibetan monastic orders and the size, splendor and magnificence of so many of their former communities now appear to be a part of Tibet's past. Since the coming of the Chinese, priceless libraries have reportedly been burned, monasteries looted, orders of Buddhist monks and nuns roughly disbanded. Many of the great lamas have fled to other lands, if not to save their lives, then—what is far more important to them personally—in the hope of preserving ancient and revered teachings. Certainly the basic tenet of the Buddha's *Dharma*, that all life is in a constant condition of flux, that there is no lasting permanence to be found in the material universe, has been demonstrated on a very large scale in Tibet's recent history. Yet, on the positive side, the arrival of the Chinese has undoubtedly contributed in a major way to the spread of the *Dharma* not only through parts of Asia but in Europe and America as well.

An impressive tribute to the strength of Tibetan Buddhism is the manner in which refugees have managed to keep vitally alive the practice of their religion in new surroundings where grim discomfort and even deprivation are so often their lot. The Dalai Lama himself, essentially their pope, lives in northern India in a modest bungalow, while scattered through the countries of the lower Himalayas, and in India also, there are innumerable small groups of his displaced subjects sharing together their few worldly possessions and, with undimmed loyalty and a good heart, continuing daily practice of a magnificent faith which came to its full growth in the isolated, awesome land that has often been called the world's rooftop.

Anyone who has spent time among the homeless but resolutely cheerful Tibetan people in exile, or even casually encountered them, cannot fail to be impressed by their adaptability and stout-heartedness. Many travelers have spoken of the amazing spirit with which —given only a leaky shelter, a little rice and a cake of compressed tea—ordinary Tibetans continue their spiritual practices. Ritual disciplines are organized, bells ring, the tremendous monastery horns are again blown and the rare organlike voices, so unique to Tibetan chanting, can be heard.

A definite semblance of formal life-structure has, of course, been painstakingly built up around the present circumscribed existence of the Dalai Lama, the most honored and world-famous of a number of eminent Tibetan religious personages who, before recent events dispersed them from their homeland, were entirely unknown to the West, even by title. Although the modest headquarters of the Dalai Lama in Dharmsala, India, is a very far cry from the famed magnificence of the Potala in Lhasa, power radiates from this lively Center. In 1971 a library of Tibetan Works and Archives was established to become a repository of whatever precious materials —manuscripts, books, icons, *thankas* (religious paintings)—had been saved by fleeing Tibetans. The Dharmsala Center not only publishes a scholarly periodical, *The Tibet Journal*, it also offers authoritative courses in Tibetan Buddhism and the Tibetan language. In the relatively few years since the Center's founding, many foreign students from America, Europe and Japan have taken advantage of the opportunity to study near the source of Tibet's long-unknown and now imperiled culture.

In keeping with the Buddhist belief in the importance of an oral tradition—the imparting of knowledge by word of mouth from master to disciple—the Dharmsala Center also makes use of an "unrecorded storehouse" of wisdom still to be found in the minds and memories of Tibetan teachers. Because a part of Tibet's oral tradition has always consisted of related folk tales and songs, these vital links with Tibet's past are being preserved in a formal and scholarly Oral History Project designed to protect and transmit a matchless heritage to younger generations growing up far removed from their cultural roots. There is even instruction in the traditional art of *thanka* painting by artists trained in the exacting techniques of preparing paints and surfaces and the detailed iconography of these sacred scrolls which play such an important part in Tibetan religious instruction. *Thankas* represent schematic or symbolic maps of psychological energies and mental qualities, thus serving as aids in certain Tibetan meditation practices.

Unquestionably, the most meaningful result of the mass exodus of Tibetans from their country has been the acceptance on the part of certain *rinpoches* (exalted teachers) of their roles as carriers of Tibetan Buddhism to the West. This unexpected destiny, growing out of dismaying loss and disruption, is exemplified by the presence in America of a growing number of highly qualified teachers. In a surprisingly short time, there have gathered around these teachers large groups of eager students to whom many of the practices cited above are being transmitted.

One of the most influential older writers and scholars among the contemporary Tibetan Buddhists to visit the West in recent years is Lama Anagarika Govinda, now living and teaching at a Zen center in northern California. Lama Govinda describes himself as an "Indian national of European descent and Buddhist faith belonging to a Tibetan Order and believing in the brotherhood of man." In *The Foundations of Tibetan Mysticism* Govinda relates a story about his own guru, Tomo Geshe, which sheds light on the purpose behind the recent voluntary Western exile of so many brilliant Tibetans. Govinda's guru had for many years lived the life of a religious recluse in a remote mountain hermitage far removed from other human beings. Abruptly one day he abandoned his prolonged contemplative solitude because of a vivid vision of humanity's growing desperate plight.

In this vision Tomo Geshe had seen all mankind standing at the crossroads of a fateful choice. One road represented the Path of Power so suddenly opened up by science's discovery of long-hidden secrets of nature. This way of power, if not understood and controlled, would inescapably lead mankind to self-destruction.

There was, however, in Tomo Geshe's vision an alternative road for man to take: the Path of Enlightenment, whose goal was the acquiring of deeper knowledge and control of the equally mysterious, still untapped forces *that lie within the human being himself*; energies capable of leading humanity away from destruction toward eventual "liberation and self-realization." Tomo Geshe conceived his remaining life task to be the offering of personal assistance in the following of this latter path.

It seems safe to assume that Lama Govinda's appearance in Europe and America expresses a concern similar to that of his guru, as do also the teaching centers now firmly established in the United States by Chögyam Trungpa, Tarthung Tulku and a number of other transplanted *rinpoches*. In a 1974 issue of *Crystal Mirror*, the periodical issued by Tarthung Tulku's group in Berkeley (the Nyingma Meditation Center), this *rinpoche* wrote:

> With the current growth of man's power over both his world and his fellow man, it is particularly desirable that this power be tempered with an understanding of man's nature, of what is possible and what is appropriate to him. The theory and practice of Vajrayana Buddhism are connected in the most incisive and practical way possible with such understanding and are therefore capable of making significant contributions to the resolution of man's present problems and the realization of his potential for future growth.

As a background to the growing interest in Tibetan Buddhism in the West, it seems relevant to consider some of the religious customs and beliefs of the world's last great theocracy.

Among the most fundamental and commonplace of Tibetan religious beliefs is reincarnation, the doctrine that a man lives more than one life (as already noted, a basic tenet of Hindu and Buddhist metaphysics in general). Tibet has made special contributions to this doctrine by establishing among its religious leaders the principle of succession by reincarnation. A part of this teaching includes the recognition of *tulkus*, children who are identified when still quite young as specific reincarnations of noted religious personages. The Dalai Lama is the most famed of these significant incarnations, but the title *tulku* has been held by a long series of heads of monastic establishments and many individual teachers bearing such other honorifics as lama or *rinpoche*. The number of recognized *tulkus* in Tibet (and still presumably being born among Tibetan exiles) is variously reckoned at "around three hundred" or "several thousand." (Under existing conditions no accurate figure seems possible to come by, and it is perhaps unimportant.)

The discovery or recognition of a *tulku* comes early in the life of a child: often between the years of two and five. The brother of the present Dalai Lama, Thubten Jigme Norbu, now an American citizen, was recognized as a *tulku* some years before the formal recognition of his renowned younger sibling. Norbu relates in his autobiography, *Tibet Is My Country*, that before he was eight, he was "confirmed as the reincarnation of a high-ranking monk named Tegster," and by the age of ten had been transported from his humble farming home to the great monastery at Kumbum to embark on a monastic career which was abruptly terminated by the arrival of the Communist Chinese. Similarly, Chögyam Trungpa, Rinpoche, the distinguished head of several Tibetan Buddhist meditation centers in America, tells us in an introductory note to a new edition of The Tibetan Book of the Dead that he received his special "transmission" at the age of eight and was thereafter trained by his tutors in the understanding of "the process of death." This training necessitated his visiting the dying on an average of four times a week, "so that the notion of impermanence would become a living experience rather than a philosophical view." (We will return further on to Tibetan Buddhist doctrines on death.)

When a *tulku* is discovered or "recognized," his qualifications for advanced spiritual training and eventual leadership are carefully checked by religious authorities. Various tests of confirmation are put to him, or her, for, significantly, female *tulkus* as well as male are recognized by Tibetans. Among the standard tests is the child's ability to select, from a miscellany of objects presented him, those once in the possession of his deceased predecessor—in other words, his own property in a former life. After official confirmation the young *tulku* embarks on a period of strict training and specific guidance designed as a preparation for the responsible position he will actively fill in maturity.

Young *tulkus* (whom some Western writers have unfortunately chosen to designate as "living Buddhas") often astonish non-Tibetans by the extraordinary maturity, dignity and inner quiet shown by them at an early age. The daughter of a chief interpreter for the Dalai Lama is a recognized *tulku*, and because of her status she has always received a great deal of homage, yet Westerners who met her as a child were invariably impressed by how "unspoiled" she was. A combination of easy buoyant naturalness and an exceptional kind of attentive composure appears to be characteristic of all these remarkable children.

I myself was once presented to a very young "reincarnated lama." He was brought by an escort of elderly monks, fleeing from the Chinese, to the door of a house in Kalimpong where I was staying. The little boy's guardians, all of them travel-worn and exhausted but plainly devoted to their precious charge, wanted advice on where to deliver their little *tulku* so that he might learn to speak English. The boy was five years old at the most, yet his perceptive gaze, his adult dignity and poise, conveyed an arresting sense of timeless wisdom, an acute mature awareness at once detached and compassionate. I have never forgotten his beautiful face and his bearing, which, in spite of his chronological age, could only be described as noble.

Arnaud Desjardins, a Frenchman who in recent years penetrated deeply into Tibetan religious traditions while traveling in Himalayan lands, was particularly struck with the effectiveness of the Tibetan *tulku* system by which superior human beings are found and educated. Quite apart from its arcane aspects, the system seemed to exemplify for him a positive way of ensuring gifted children a chance to grow up outside a family environment where conditions of either deprivation or overindulgence could well prevent a prodigy from developing his fullest capacities.

In spite of his deep respect, even reverence, for Buddhist teachings, Desjardins has "adhered," as he expresses it, to his own faith, Christianity; but he cannot resist the temptation to wonder what it would be like if the theory of reincarnated Great Teachers were a part of Christian belief. As a matter of historical fact, the theory of reincarnation was accepted by Christians until the Council of Constantinople held in A.D. 551, and the Bible offers researchers in this subject a number of relevant passages. In his book *The Message of the Tibetans*, Desjardins speculates:

Let us imagine that on the death of St. Bernard of Clairvaux, or St. Francis of Assisi, the Cistercian and Franciscan monks had sought to recognize in what other human being the impulse of active wisdom or of boundless compassion which these Founders of their Orders had manifested in the flesh was going to manifest itself again, and that even today Christendom could present us somewhere and in some physical form with the real St. Bernard or St. Francis.

For many centuries, the locating of a new Dalai Lama has followed a specific formula similar to the discovery of any *tulku*, only in the case of this most eminent of all Tibetan religious figures the search has been conducted expressly and formally by the Regents of Tibet. On the death of the incumbent Dalai Lama the State Oracle has been consulted for a preliminary reading on the geographic region where his successor should be sought. A guiding vision, a directive "picture," has been looked for in a lake sacred to the Goddess Kali, an Indian deity said to have appeared to the first of the many Dalai Lamas with the promise to watch over successive incarnations. The vision seen in the depths of this sacred body of water provides the Regents with further clues to the specific geographic direction in which they should travel on their crucial expedition. An official search party is then organized, its members carefully disguised to appear as a simple band of pilgrims while they make their anonymous journey, often to remote parts of their sparsely settled, wild and mountainous land.

In the case of the present Dalai Lama, the fourteenth in succession of his line, His Holiness was found when still a child, living on his family's farm in the far eastern district of Amdo. When the search party—ostensibly, it should be remembered, only a small group of traveling pilgrims, a common enough sight in Tibet in former times—arrived at the Norbu farmhouse, the little boy who was destined to play such an exalted role in Tibetan history amazed his parents by running to greet their visitors with all the open joy of someone encountering old familiar friends.

Traditional tests of his true identity were then put to the child, who, like his older *tulku* brother, Jigme Norbu, had been born in a cow byre. From among the rosaries shown him he chose, without hesitation, the one that belonged to his predecessor—in the Tibetan view, actually his own. He also selected unerringly from among a number of counterfeits the former Dalai Lama's personal walking staff and drum. Further, to everyone's astonishment, he was able to recite a certain six-syllabled *mantra* sacred to the *Bodhisattva* of Compassion (Avalokiteshvara), whose incarnation each successive Dalai Lama is believed to be. In short, the young child easily passed every test to which he was put, thus offering impressive proof of his former identity. But because this ordination would be of such importance to the spiritual and material well-being of every Tibetan in the land, the State Oracle had to be consulted on several more occasions before any final binding decision was made.

The exciting days of search, discovery and eventual confirmation of a new Dalai Lama, along with the ceremonies following his installation, were, in the past, the high points of the Tibetan—in particular, the city of Lhasa's—social and religious calendar. For the young Dalai Lama, however, even after his formal installation, many years of the most demanding intellectual and spiritual discipline lay ahead until at last, through his own efforts, the title of Doctor of Literature and Philosophy (*geshe*) could be fairly awarded. Not until he completed his long period of exacting preliminary training would he be permitted to devote himself to the deeper study and practice of the Tantrayana, the "flower of Tibetan Buddhism." Further intensive training, countless hours of disciplined meditation, and prolonged periods of retreat brought him at last to the place where he was ready to be acclaimed "Master of the School of Wisdom and Holder of the Wheel of the Buddha Dharma."

In this elevated position, ruling from the fortress palace of the Potala in Lhasa, every Dalai Lama has concerned himself with the quiet propagation of Buddhism in general and, in particular, the teaching of the *Gelugpa*, or the so-called Yellow-Hat School. This School is the youngest of the four main branches of Tibetan Buddhism, dating back to the fourteenth century. It is as head of this Order that the Dalai Lama governs, even in exile, the Tibetan people.

In addition to the *Gelugpa* (Yellow-Hats), there are three other important Tibetan schools: the *Kargyupa* (or Red-Hats), the *Nyingmapa* (or the Ancients) and the *Sakyapa*.* (The syllable *pa* means merely the "people" of a certain provenance.) These three latter orders are reputedly less given to erudition than the Yellow-Hat *Gelugpa*. They are said to place book learning somewhat below the direct experiential practice of their beliefs. *All such distinctions must, of course, be considered relative.* Actually, there are many noted scholars in the sects of every Tibetan Buddhist school. In fact, it is claimed that the Kargyupa, down the years, have produced as many commentaries and translations as the Gelugpa. For example, Tibet's greatest national poetry, the Songs of Milarepa, is a part of the Kargyu tradition and the extraordinary scripture known as the Tibetan Book of the Dead belongs, so to speak, to the Nyingma.

Although the Yellow-Hats, headed by the Dalai Lama, represent the formal governing body of the church in Tibet, it is important to keep in mind that Tibetans have always had free access to the teachers and teaching of any sect or school which suited their

---

* So-called because this sect's first monastery was built on a patch of gray-colored earth (*sa-kya*). (See Kenneth Morgan, *The Path of the Buddha*, Chapter 6.)

position in life and their specific personal needs. This significant characteristic springs not only from the average Tibetan's ingrained tolerance but also from the general Buddhist attitude that different people require different methods by which to deepen their spiritual consciousness. In Buddhism, various ways of approach to eventual enlightenment are not graded as superior or inferior, good or bad, but simply as different. One man's "skillful means" will not necessarily meet the requirements of another.

The unusual willingness of the Tibetans to honor varying spiritual methods and beliefs, not only within their own tradition but in the traditions of strangers to their culture, has always been one of the notable traits of these exceptional people. Marco Pallis, in *Peaks and Lamas*, has described the puzzlement of proselytizing European missionaries as far back as the seventeenth century, when Tibet was briefly opened to Western influence. The warmth of the welcome these zealous Christians received led them to a somewhat mistaken optimism about making converts. Pallis remarks:

> The Tibetans are always ready to offer worship to any sacred object and do not necessarily confine their homage to the more familiar forms. They do not feel that by so doing they are tacitly admitting to the superiority of the foreign tradition or showing infidelity towards their own. They will bow as naturally before a crucifix as they would at the feet of the Buddha, whereas our own people, accustomed to the sectarian exclusiveness of Europe, usually feel that by offering reverence in a church with the tenets of which they disagree they are condoning errors.

Marco Pallis also tells us that this notable freedom from "spiritual immaturity" not only was found in the past—when it was the custom for strangers meeting along the Chinese-Tibetan border to ask after the first formal greeting, "Sir, and to which sublime tradition do you belong?"—but continues among Tibetans to the present day.

Desjardins, too, has a number of stories that illustrate Tibetan ecumenism at the highest level. He had gone out to India in the hope of traveling in lands adjacent to Tibet and among the Tibetan refugees in order to record for French television whatever he could find of legendary religious disciplines and rituals. His plan of travel necessitated, not alone getting permission from the Indian government (which has established strictly defined military limits for travelers in this part of the world) but, even more difficult, or so he anticipated, permission from the Dalai Lama (whose word is still law with Tibetans of all sects) respectfully to explore certain arcane teachings usually kept from outsiders. Desjardins had been well briefed on the physical hazards involved in his strenuous journey. He also realized how sophisticated Tibetans, above all Tibet's leading prelate, might be wary of a foreigner's possible misinterpretation of their most sacred beliefs and cultural practices. It was therefore with some trepidation that he went to present his petition to the Dalai Lama. After stating his plans and his desires Desjardins found himself regarded in total silence for several long minutes with a steady disconcertingly penetrating gaze, "man to man." Then abruptly, without further questioning, warnings or restrictions of any kind, quite as if His Holiness had found out what he needed to know during this sustained wordless appraisal, he merely nodded his head and uttered the single syllable, "Yes." This simple affirmative permitted the petitioner total freedom to witness secret religious rituals and to interview, in his own way, any famous Teacher to whom his interpreter could get him entrée. This striking simplicity and openness characterized the behavior of the Dalai Lama on his first trip to America in 1979.

Similar striking examples of trust and open-mindedness toward an alien nonbeliever were evidenced to this same French traveler on several occasions. One in particular deserves mention, since it took place on a visit to the Gyalwa Karmapa, the highly revered head of the Kargyu Sect dwelling at a monastery near Gangtok in Sikkim. (The Karmapa's trips to the United States have made his name familiar to many Americans who attended, or read newspaper accounts of, his public performance of the Vajra Crown, "Black Hat," Ceremony.* His visit to the Hopi Indians of the Southwest,

---

* Explanations of the true significance of the formal donning of this ancient sacred headgear are not easily come by; the story of the Crown is embedded in a web of historical and mythological interpretations. In the simplest terms it might be said that through this ritualistic act the Karmapa seeks to convey and awaken a unifying sense of the all-embracing compassionate wisdom of the great *Bodhisattva*, Avalokiteshvara.

where he was reported to have helped bring rain during a serious drought, was also well publicized.)

During several informative interviews with this impressive religious personage at his Sikkim monastery, the French visitor had been struck by the genial prelate's warmth and candor. He had also been impressed by the egoless ease with which the Karmapa could admit unfamiliarity, even ignorance, about certain basic doctrinal questions couched in Western terminology. Occasionally His Holiness might ask an assistant to get him further information; just as often he would concede, without the slightest embarrassment or defensiveness, that the subject was outside his personal range of knowledge or, for that matter, his personal interest. There was no attempt whatsoever on his part to proselytize for Buddhism. When, in fact, the Karmapa made his French visitor a gift of the *dorje* (thunderbolt) and bell sacred to Tantric initiation, he did so with the disarming statement that although similar objects could be purchased in any Darjeeling antique shop, he was presenting this particular bell and *dorje* to "honor" his guest's "non-Buddhist initiation." In his brief speech of presentation the Karmapa announced that he was by this gift paying special respect to Desjardins for "remaining faithful to yourself and refusing to let it be thought that you are prepared to recognize the superiority of Buddhism and that you are considering being converted. You have maintained that attitude because you believe that *Truth is greater than religion*."

Tibetan Buddhism is referred to today under the name *Tantrayana* or *Vajrayana*. In common usage the terms seem virtually interchangeable. *Vajrayana* derives from the Sanskrit word *vajra*—in the Tibetan tongue *dorje*, usually translated into English as "thunderbolt." The *dorje* or *vajra* is a sacred object which often appears in Tibetan ritual and art. Lama Govinda strenuously objects to the Western translation of *dorje* as thunderbolt, insisting that no such association exists in the Tibetan Buddhist tradition. Instead, he prefers to equate the *vajra* with the diamond, or the "king of stones," and translates *Vajrayana* as The Way of the Diamond Scepter, "capable of cutting asunder any other substance but which itself cannot be cut by anything."

The term *Tantrayana* also suffers from general Western misconceptions about the origin and significance of Tantrism as practiced by Tibetan Buddhists. Many of the common assumptions about its practices have their source directly or indirectly in lurid accounts by traveling "authorities" of the past, who, like I. A. Waddell, have equated Tantrism with "demon worship" and "black magic," condemning it as "a parasite whose monster outgrowth crushed and cancered most of the little life of purely Buddhist stock left in Mahayana."

There has been considerable disagreement among scholars as to the origins and genesis of Tantrism—a controversy which need not concern us here. Whatever its true source, Tantrism in both India and Tibet did develop two main branches: the so-called Right-hand Path, characterized by profound philosophy and strict disciplines, and the Left-hand Path, whose followers emphasize ceremonies ("enactment"), direct experience (often of conflict), and sometimes ritualistic sexual practices. (Indian Tantrism is related to the worship of the god Shiva and his female principle, or *shakti*.)

Western resistance to Tantrism often focuses on certain forms of religious art, in particular the image commonly known as *yab-yum*, which represents a man and a woman in an act of intimate sexual congress. Sometimes referred to as "Father-Mother pairs," these statues—which have no prurient connotation for Tibetans—are intended to express the inseparable qualities of Enlightenment: wisdom, tranquillity and bliss. Fosco Maraini in *Secret Tibet* has written compellingly of the effect on a Western observer of confrontation with these sacred images in the gloom of a Tibetan temple:

It is truly an impressive experience to penetrate into the stuffy and venerable darkness of a temple, where the silence seems to be a positive thing, having a solidity and a consistency of its own, and there, in its innermost depths, on a golden altar, among dragons, lotus flowers, brocades, peacock feathers, the flickering of butter burning in tiny cups, and butter worked into elaborate shapes and patterns for offerings, to find oneself face to face with the Absolute, the Ultimate, the First, the Eternal, the Everlasting, and the All-Pervading, in the form of a bejewelled prince voluptuously embracing his own shakti.

What fantastic imagination, what metaphysical daring, to represent the most abstract possible concept, a concept definable only by negatives, like mathematical infinity, by the most concrete, the most carnal picture that it is possible to imagine; to symbolize that which is without beginning and without end by that which is *par excellence* ephemeral and fugitive; to identify extreme serenity with extreme passion, the crystal light of the stars with the fire of love, the invisible and the intangible with the intoxication of all the senses; and to recall the oneness of the universe, to awareness of which the mind only rarely attains, as a result of supreme effort, in a flash of illumination, by a representation of the moment in which all thought is lost in the most complete annihilation.

Quite apart from an excusable ignorance of the esoteric significance of this ancient icon, it seems odd to many Himalayan Buddhists that strangers to their culture should find "obscene" or "repellent" such representations of that profoundly sacred, mysterious yet universal act by which all human life comes into existence. But whether from deference to the sensitivities of visitors or to protect the symbol from irreverent eyes, it is quite usual now in private shrine rooms of Himalayan Buddhism to find this icon shrouded in cloth or hidden away behind a screen.

Today the word *Tantrayana* has with amazing speed entered the vocabularies of young Westerners interested in Asian philosophies —a phenomenon not easily accounted for, since, as late as the sixties, it was difficult to find reliable writings on the subject in any European language. Now it is becoming so commonplace that, as one author recently remarked, "We may soon expect *'Tantrism in Twelve Easy Lessons'* or a *'Christian Tantrism with the Imprimatur.'* "

*Figures of couples in passionate sexual embrace are a familiar part of the religious iconography of the Himalayan world. Often misunderstood and misinterpreted, this Tantric icon (yab-yum) is nonprurient in intention. It is designed not merely to suggest the profound mystery of human union, but the attainment of the inseparable qualities of Enlightenment—a nondualistic state of wisdom and bliss. Nepal. Fifteenth century. Silver with polychrome.*

Certainly Tantrayana (or Vajrayana) as commonly taught today by qualified Tibetan Buddhists seems, at least in its public aspects, rather far removed from the lurid accounts of Tantrism in sensationalized books. It is quite easy to find clear statements of purpose and direction made by leading Tibetan Tantric teachers now in America. One example taken at random should suffice to make the point. In the magazine *Garuda IV*, writing on "The Foundations of Mindfulness," Chögyam Trungpa, Rinpoche has said:

People in all ages have been under stress and have devised and tried various means to escape from it only to find to their dismay that the stress did not disappear but reasserted itself in other forms as threatening as before, if not worse. This shows that escape is never an answer to the basic question of how to be a human being. Escape, whether it is the mechanical uniformity and monotony of social conformity or into a fictitious world of some transcendental make-believe, is but an admission of having failed in the ever-present task of growing up.

This forthright statement of the universal problem of escapism should not be taken to mean that attaining maturity in the terms of Tantrayana is an easy task. The concepts and practices of Tantrism are exacting and demanding. No one has stated with greater precision and dignity the Tibetan Buddhist interpretation of Tantrayana's true meaning than Lama Govinda, who tells us that the word "tantra" is related to the concept of weaving and to such other derivative terms as "thread," "web," "fabric." Originally a Sanskrit word, it refers to the warp of basic threads on which the weft is woven to become the cloth. Tantrism is, in essence, therefore, a teaching typically Buddhist, stressing as it does "the interwovenness of things and action, the interdependence of all that exists, the continuity in the interaction of cause and effect"; in other words the foundation of all action, the law and principles by which everything operates.

Tibetan Tantrayana aims to bring about the realization that the dynamic forces of the universe at large are no different from those of the individual human being. Transformation of these universal forces by the power of one's own mind (i.e., specifically through the faithful practice of meditation) is prescribed not only for the good of one's own self, but of all life—of which one is an inseparable part. In Buddhist Tantrayana, again to quote Govinda, the external and the internal worlds are in a sense "two sides of the same fabric in which threads of all forces and all events, of all forms of consciousness and of their objects are woven into an inseparable net of endless mutually conditioning relation." (This again reminds one of the Kegon Buddhists' concept of Indra's Net, described on page 54.) Tantrayana might be defined, therefore, as a form of training designed to bring the practitioner to understand fully "the inner relationship of all things: the parallelism of microcosm and macrocosm, mind and universe, ritual and reality, the world of matter and the world of spirit."

A simple way—at least on the surface—of practicing a Tantric attitude toward life is suggested in a book by John Blofeld,* an Englishman who has spent the major part of his lifetime studying

---

* *The Tantric Mysticism of Tibet*, John Blofeld, E. P. Dutton & Co., New York, 1970.

Buddhist disciplines in various parts of Asia and writing about them with commendable clarity for a large Western readership. Blofeld tells us that one of his lama teachers, an honored Mongolian *geshe*, which is to say an exceptionally well-qualified exponent of Buddhist *Dharma*, began his personal instruction by expounding the inner meaning of certain significant scriptural passages. The statements on which Blofeld was asked to meditate were three in number: "See everything around you as Nirvana. See all beings as the Buddha. Hear all sounds as mantra [sacred]."

The recognition of "everything around one as Nirvana" might be said to be the supreme goal of Buddhist endeavor, as it indicates release from the limitations of human existence, without, however, any unnatural repudiation of that existence. In Tantrayana the world of *samsara* is not something we leave behind in order to enter another realm, that of nirvana; the realms are essentially one. It is our own faculty of misperception which makes them appear different, but this faculty can be altered through an intensification in consciousness comparable to the kind of mind change reported by many people who, under the influence of drugs like LSD, have become vividly aware of something they can describe only as "Isness," an adequate translation of *Tathagata*—the name for Buddha in the largest sense. This tremendous reality, though impossible to formulate in concrete descriptive terms, is, however, perceived as overwhelmingly beautiful and sacred.

The disciple in the Tantrayana (or Vajrayana) tradition does not, of course, depend on drugs for this kind of revelation. The development comes about through the persistent, directed practice of ever deepening meditation. Meditation is considered the one and only sure way to "an altered state of consciousness," a condition once described by Chögyam Trungpa as "basic sanity."

On the prime importance of meditation as a means of comprehending reality all Buddhists agree, for the mind, our mind, is the real culprit, or magician; it is the mind which makes us believe that the illusory world is "true." Blofeld cites a very commonplace occurrence which exemplified for him, in the simplest terms, the working of illusion on the physical plane; the fact that beauty and its opposite are merely creations of the mind. To his delight while out riding one day he had seen at a distance masses of scarlet blossoms on a clump of green trees. Coming abreast of this exquisitely beautiful sight, he was astonished to find only a corrugated zinc fence with a coating of bright red lead standing in front of some trees. The scene had not changed, merely his, the observer's, viewpoint; an experience not unlike those desert mirages so compellingly described by Antoine de Saint-Exupéry in *Wind, Sand, and Stars* which led him to question physical "reality" as a fixed principle of reference.

The *geshe*'s second admonition to Blofeld, "to practice seeing all beings as Buddha," was designed not alone to aid in eventual perception of the "undifferentiated Isness" of the universe but also to stimulate the recognition that every sentient being (including one's "self") is already sharing in and capable of attaining the final state of Enlightenment, or Buddhahood. Naturally while working at this exercise of seeing everything as the Buddha, the practitioner would show loving-kindness, compassion and respect to everyone who crossed his path.

As for the *geshe*'s further stipulation, "Hear all sounds as mantra," the author again draws on a personal experience as illustration. After a prolonged sojourn in a remote Tibetan monastery where he was accustomed to meditate to the soothing and stirring sounds of Tibetan music heard above a nearby waterfall, he had taken up residence in Bangkok in a house on a noisy street. Here, outside his window, during his morning meditation hour boys driving motor-tricycle taxis in low gear were receiving loud instruction on how to handle their tricky vehicles in heavy city traffic. Just how Blofeld succeeded in transposing this cacophony into "sacred" sound may not be entirely clear to the reader, but the fact that he could do so should prove heartening to all decible-distracted city dwellers.

Blofeld does offer a helpful suggestion for the aspirant still at the level of "relative truth," which is to say when still unable to avoid making distinctions and differentiations between an ordinary human being and a Buddha, between sights that are beautiful and those that are commonplace or ugly, noises that are agreeable and those that are discordant and so on. At this point the seeker, says

Blofeld, might simply attempt to act "as if" he had already attained nondualistic perception. In its early stage of practice this "as if" may seem very much like a childish game, but this enactment is fundamental to Tantric practice and does, in Blofeld's view, help to discipline the mind and in time bring about a change in consciousness.

Although he has gone to considerable pains to simplify the instructions of his teacher, Blofeld is also careful to add a grave warning: it would be a highly dangerous mistake to assume that in the early stages of Tantric discipleship, on the way to the realization of the holiness of all things and all acts, one can with impunity discard every rule of moral or ethical behavior on the grounds that there is no such duality as good and evil or that "passion must be given free rein to destroy passion." In truth, to overcome the sense of the "opposites," to transcend dualism, requires unswerving effort, dedication and integrity. A profound mystical truth, not a license for unbridled appetite, is expressed in the Sanskrit Tantric aphorism *sarvam annam*, "Everything is food." To be sure, say the Tantrists, everything can nourish us, all experiences, sense impressions, feelings, thoughts. What determines their effect on us is our use of them. Tantrayana attempts to create a conscious connection between the events of daily existence and so-called spiritual experience. A process known as "transformation" is therefore fundamental to the Tantric Buddhist Way.

Because of the clear dangers of misinterpretation inherent in the very nature of many Tantric practices, however, Tantrayana strongly emphasizes the necessity of finding a responsible personal guru and receiving individual teacher-to-pupil instructions suited to one's character and capabilities or, one might say, to one's present place on the Path. So important in Tibetan Buddhism is the idea of the personal guru that to the traditional Buddhist formulation of the Three Treasures, the Buddha, the Teaching (*Dharma*) and the Community of Monks (the *Sangha*), Tibetans add a fourth "treasure," one's own guru.

The word "guru," originating in Hinduism but now become a part of the English vocabulary, is generally translated as "teacher," but this is not an equivalent term. In *The Way of the White Clouds*

Lama Govinda says: "A teacher gives knowledge but a guru gives himself." He goes on to explain that the real teachings of a guru are not conveyed through what he says but through his physical presence; what he represents in his total being goes beyond the power of human speech. The guru is an "inspirer" in the truest sense of the word; one who infuses the *chela,* or disciple, with his own living spirit so that the aim toward which the disciple is striving changes from a mere vague ideal to an experienced reality seen in the person of his spiritual guide.

Dr. Herbert V. Guenther, who coauthored *The Dawn of Tantra* with Chögyam Trungpa, has expressed the guru-*chela* relation in a somewhat different way. He says that "properly used, this term does not refer so much to a human person as to the object of a shift in attention which takes place from the human person who imparts the teaching to the teaching itself." Guenther goes on to suggest that the guru might properly be called "a spiritual friend," and he adds these significant and clarifying words: "one who is able to impart spiritual guidance *because he has been through the process himself*" [italics added].

Whatever the true interpretation of the word "guru," it represents an idea which has long seemed alien to the Western spirit. The modern acceptability of this once-suspect term by so many "East Turners" (as Harvey Cox has called them in his book *Turning East*), as well as by those who calmly accept the honor of the title, represents an interesting phenomenon of the present era. Gurus of every kind now seem increasingly available in the West, often under very unlikely circumstances. Authenticating the guru might be said to be a new challenge in the Occident, where this particular religious tradition is new and relatively untried.

Tibetans have always impressed foreigners with their remarkably objective, one might even say "scientific," attitude toward many kinds of phenomena to which we in the West would assign occult or psychic significance. To Tibetan Tantrists who believe in life's interacting, interwoven web of which man is a part and whose common laws he shares, it follows that there are specifically gifted or trained people who understand and can consciously participate in such phenomena. It has been suggested that the calm Tibetan attitude toward spectacular control of certain forms of energy, to us baffling and inexplicable, could be compared to our quite matter-of-fact acceptance of that mysterious force we call electricity. Because of its familiarity, we put electricity to use daily without any special thought or understanding and certainly without in any way connecting it with "religion." So, although teaching about "magical" powers and practices is not an intrinsic part of the most profound Buddhist teaching (the Buddha always minimized the development or display of supramundane capabilities), certain Tibetan Buddhists do unquestionably make use of paranormal energies.

An example or two may indicate something of Tantric utilization of the untapped physical capacities of the human body. Trustworthy Western observers have given witness to the ability of Tibetan initiates to withstand extremes of unrelieved cold, including total immersion in the icy waters of high mountain lakes, in temperatures well below freezing, with no ill effects—in fact, without even seeming to feel the cold. This power comes from training in the yoga of Psychic Heat or Inner Fire, known as *tum-mo*. It is knowledge of how to rouse this bodily heat and sustain it which has made it possible for hermits in deep meditation to endure Tibetan winters in unheated caves high in the mountains. Part of the strenuous training needed to achieve *tum-mo* consists of the daily practice of wrapping one's body in a succession of sheets dipped in ice water which the neophyte must dry rapidly through his inner heat.

It is tempting to dwell on examples of the exceptional powers Tibetans have been reported as able to develop through various practices combining special powers of concentration, breathing exercises and yogic or gymnastic training. Tibet's reputation for the development among its holy men of extraordinary thaumaturgic powers has long been a part of Tibetan arcane lore. The appetite for anecdotes about this side of Tibetan life has been fed by such books as *The Third Eye*,* which appeared some years ago, creating a great stir in a wide readership as it purported to be an

* By T. Lobsang Rampa (pseudonym for C. H. Hoskin), New York, Doubleday & Co., 1957.

authentic account of various superhuman physical feats described by an avowed ex-lama.

Most of the sensational stories of impressionable writers are not difficult to put aside. It is, however, not so easy to dismiss the first-hand experiences of such a distinguished scholar-observer as Alexandra David-Neel. In *With Mystics and Magicians in Tibet* she offers her readers some almost incredible anecdotes about the amazing feats of certain Tantric initiates. She describes at some length the special powers of the *lung-gom-pa*, or "wind men," who after years of strenuous practice and extremes of physical discipline have succeeded in freeing themselves of certain bodily limitations, enabling them to travel, so it is claimed, "hundreds of miles in a single day." During her many years in Tibet, Madame David-Neel saw only three of these adepts. One, moving with incredible swiftness, passed her and her caravan without seeming to see them. He appeared to be traveling in a trance; his face calm and impassive, his wide-open eyes fixed far ahead in space. She had been warned by a member of her party not to speak because of the possible shock it would cause, but she was near enough to observe, as he passed, that he was carrying under his cloak a *phurba*, or magic dagger. With its point held down toward the ground, he appeared to be leaning on it as if it was a staff helping to propel him at superhuman speed over the rough terrain.

She has also described the achievements of one who has taken training in levitation. A successful candidate in this exacting discipline must learn to leap, while seated in a cross-legged position, twice his body height, through a small aperture at the top of a cupola built over the pit in which he is seated. Such spectacular feats follow years of training in breathing exercises, practiced in

*Tara. The gracious figure of Tara, a representation in Himalayan iconography (i.e., Nepal, Bhutan, Tibet) of the Bodhisattva Avalokiteshvara. Gilt bronze. Nepal. Fifteenth–sixteenth century.*

*Seated Buddha. Another representation of the Buddha of the Future, Maitreya. This one, Tibetan, is seated in conventional yogic posture, while his hands make the gesture known as "Turning the Wheel of the Law." Thirteenth–fourteenth century.*

strict seclusion, also in complete darkness. What is achieved is essentially weightlessness which, David-Neel was told, should enable the "graduate" to sit on an ear of barley without bending its stalk or to stand at the top of a heap of grain without displacing any of it.

This same redoubtable Buddhist traveler—who, although a woman and a foreigner, was treated with great respect by the many learned scholars she encountered in her travels through Tibet, Sikkim and elsewhere in the Himalayan world—has also reported witnessing, quite by chance, the training required by a monk learning to use psychophysical powers to help the "spirit" of a dying man leave its body through the top of the skull. A combination of controlled breathing, ritualistic cries and total motionlessness made it possible for the monk in training to open the top of his skull wide enough to permit a straw to stand upright in the aperture. This David-Neel saw herself. Later, seeking an explanation for the curious scene on which she had accidentally stumbled, it was explained that after learning to do this to himself (with observance of the strictest precautions) the monk-trainee would be able to aid the departure of the spirit of a dying person through *his* skull opening. In reading such accounts, one thinks of the possible connection with the fontanelle, or soft spot on the top of a baby's head, which gradually closes over as the child grows.

All of the above "miracles" and many others quite certainly did take place in Tibet in the past; perhaps they do even today. Madame David-Neel, however, like a good Buddhist, is careful to warn against regarding exceptional or unfamiliar physical feats as supernatural events. Most "wonders" are, to the upper ranks of Tibetan Buddhists, understood as natural events which simply result from the skillful handling of little-understood laws and forces. So-called lamas on a certain level may be guilty of responding to folk superstition with holy water, holy pills, printed charms, specially knotted scarfs and so on; on another level it is recognized that exceptional psychophysical abilities are simply the result of the knowledge and control of invisible but tangible "energies" by which we are all surrounded.

In this respect it is significant that when it comes to the selection of individuals for higher training in the use of such powers, Tibetan teachers are said to choose the most robust and down-to-earth types rather than "sensitives" or those who would appear to be specially inclined toward "spirituality." The truth seems to be that it takes exceptional physical stamina to achieve practical results, or even to survive the rigors of initiation, in these exacting yogic practices.

Of particular importance to the contemporary Western world, now obviously approaching a different understanding of death and the act of dying, is the Tibetan belief in the ritual meaning and significance of a man's last hours on earth. Part of the Tibetan tradition places special emphasis on the condition of consciousness at the time of death in the belief that the dying person's mental and emotional state will, to some degree, control his afterlife and rebirth pattern.

In Tibetan teaching the hours preceding death, and those immediately following, directly affect the sojourn in the Bardo, a dreamlike realm lying between life and death. The Bardo experience is influenced by the dying person's degree of enlightenment and also by the formal supportive services of attendant lamas, relatives and friends. The dying are exhorted to bend every effort toward release into a "consciousness free from all limitations" symbolized by the "clear light of the void," said to be visible at some point to the dying everywhere. If, however, the departing aggregate of energies is inexorably, *karmically* pulled back toward an earthly existence, then the ministrations of the attendants will assist the departing spirit toward a higher rebirth state.

Accounts of experiences considered natural to the predeath and postdeath states have been kept for centuries as a part of Tibetan Buddhism's arcane lore. The most well known of these records is The Tibetan Book of the Dead, *The Bardo Thödol*, translated by the famous Western scholar Dr. W. Y. Evans-Wentz, in collaboration with Lama Kazi Dawa-Samdup, a noted Tibetan linguist. There is also a new translation available, with an introduction by Francesca Fremantle and a valuable commentary by Chögyam Trungpa. It should be noted at the outset that this ancient Tibetan scripture is grounded in significant and deep differences between Asian and Western attitudes towards life's end, differences already spoken of in the preceding section on Theravada. We in the West tend to ignore, push aside or recoil from death. Although it is the inescapable consequence of the very fact of having been born, the subject is taboo. Some part of our unexpressed fear and repugnance must surely be related to that ego identification with body and mind which the Buddha was so interested in dispelling and which is the aim of all Buddhist meditation techniques.

Asians in general, Tibetans in particular, have an altogether different attitude toward the physical body when it is no longer occupied by its departed consciousness; in fact, they often offer corpses as a supreme act of charity to hungry birds or animals. Alexandra David-Neel has described the matter-of-factness with which two of her servants, who were also monks, once broke open a coffin found beside the road in search of the femur bones used in the making of flutes for certain Tantric rites. David-Neel did not directly protest their behavior, for she understood Tibetans, but with her Western upbringing she did feel impelled to prevent the opening of a second coffin by suggesting that there might be cholera germs lurking within. When this warning proved effective she thought to herself, in some amusement, that although as a Westerner she found it difficult to believe in invisible "demonic" powers (which naturally her servants did), she found it easy to believe in other invisible harmful energies called germs.

Tibetans' casual attitude toward corpses is, however, in marked contrast to their attentive behavior at the very hour of death and immediately after it has occurred. This behavior, quite dissimilar to ours in the West, seems to objective eyes far more civilized, for it is the Western practice to remove a body from its deathbed in crude haste, almost before it is cold, in order to embark immediately on whatever is needed to prepare it for public display, or cremation. Dehumanized hospital regulations permit no latitude for any possible "rites of passage" at this great moment when life is exchanged for death. Tibetans, on the contrary, pay special attention to such rites.

In the preface to the second edition of *The Tibetan Book of the*

*Dead,* Evans-Wentz expressed the fervent hope that his arduous scholarly efforts would in some way help the Occident to learn to practice an "Art of Dying." It is, in his view, as possible to "abort" the death process as it is to abort the birth process, and he speaks with pitying despair of the way in which "every effort is apt to be made by a materialistically inclined medical science to postpone and thereby interfere with, the death-process." He deplores the fact that so few people who are dying are permitted to remain in familiar surroundings, or when the hospital has been reached, to be left in an undisturbed state. "To die in a hospital, probably while under the mind-benumbing influence of some opiate, or else under the stimulation of some drug injected into the body to enable the dying to *cling to life as long as possible,* cannot but be productive of a very undesirable death, as undesirable as that of a shell-shocked soldier on a battlefield."

Tibetan secret teachings on the death process, teachings which allegedly date back to the eighth-century Indian-born guru Padmasambhava, are now assuming new relevance in the modern West, where the "right to die" has recently become a slogan of certain dedicated groups distressed by medicine's exaggerated emphasis on prolongation of life at all costs. Some hospitals are beginning to establish programs designed to help terminal cases face the fact of imminent death and even share with others the "act of dying,"* as Tibetans would express it.

This very expression indicates the importance Tibetans attach to conscious awareness at the hour in which physical life is terminated. In Himalayan Buddhist death rites the departing spirit is deliberately allowed ample time and peace for taking leave of its physical habitation. The necessity of maintaining "mindful" effort up to, and even after, the hour of death is stressed. Traditional meditative procedures are practiced by the dying person himself as long as possible, for in this way his individual consciousness is better able to relinquish its tenacious hold on that forever-in-flux state known as human existence. Also, in addition to the dying person's own efforts he is given the support of attendants—friends,

---

* *The Hospice Movement: A Better Way of Caring for the Dying,* Sandal Stoddard, New York, Stein and Day, 1978.

relatives, lamas—who "accompany" him on his journey, assisting him through their own meditations, to move on into the unknown without fear. It is significant that the second title of *The Tibetan Book of the Dead* is *Liberation by Hearing on the After Death Plane*.

The Tibetan Buddhist "science of dying" also stresses, with typical Buddhist psychological insight, that all the Bardo experiences, similar to dreams, visions and nightmares, are in reality merely the dead person's own thought forms. The phenomena experienced in the after-death state are related to the tastes, habits and desires of a lifetime. In Shakespeare's words:

> The whole universe is but imagination,
> all in all, is but a shadow-show
> of one's own mind.

Before concluding the subject of general Tibetan Buddhist teachings, some brief consideration must be given three of its more well-known meditation tools: mandala, *mantra* and visualization. Each of these may be taken as separate methods of Tibetan meditation practice; however, in the end they come together as a single expression of the concentrated effort of body, speech and mind in the realization of the totality of the universe and the "oneness" of self and other.

Tibetans approach the laws of sound in an objective, systematic and exact manner. They believe that the power embodied in specific sounds can set up inner vibrations which will open the mind to higher experiences. Mantrayana, or the meditative use of sacred sound, *mantra*, is the method by which this particular teaching is explored.

An etymological analysis of the Sanskrit term Mantrayana penetrates instantly to its significance. As we know from the terms Hinayana and Mahayana, a *yana* is a vessel or vehicle. The syllable *man*, related to our word "mental," connotes "to think or to have mind"; the suffix *tra* is used to form substantives denoting "instruments or tools." A *mantra* can therefore be defined as a "tool in sound," a tool designed to be used by the mind as an aid in meditation and in the eventual attainment of Buddha Wisdom. The *mantra*'s real significance involves a profound *living* experience. Only when the Buddha-nature is perceived *within* has the disciple awakened to universal enlightenment, and only then can he become an instrument for the liberation of other living beings. (A very clear analysis of *Om mani padme hum*, the classic Tibetan *mantra*, by John Blofeld can be found in Appendix I.)

Although the use of the *mantra* as an aid to meditation is very much a part of many kinds of Buddhist practice, in particular among the Tibetans and Shingon or Tantric sect of Japan, it is by no means a phenomenon unique to Buddhism. Belief in the meaning and power of sound—in even its most abstract sense—goes far back in the religious history of mankind. In the Bible there appear these arresting lines in the Gospel According to St. John: "In the beginning was the Word and the Word was with God, And the Word was God." In Hinduism as in Buddhism, chanting is a common daily practice, and one finds yogic use of sacred syllables like the all-powerful Brahmanic *Aum* (in Buddhism, *Om*). This is believed to be the first primordial sound, containing the same seminal and sustaining energy present at the origin of the universe when, in Hindu belief, creative power encapsulated in sound helped bring forth the world. The sacred word *Aum* "represents the universe in its highest and deepest aspect, in all forms and experience, which we should embrace with unlimited love and compassion like the Buddha," says Lama Govinda.

Govinda also stresses the necessity of realizing that although there is nothing innately "magical" in the knowledge and use of *mantra*, there is much more meaning in the personal utterance of holy sounds than there would be in simply playing a phonograph record of these same syllables, or in their utterance if done by someone ignorant of the *mantra*'s true significance, no matter how correct the pronunciation. Moreover, though a *mantra* may be spoken aloud, its *shabda*, or sound, is not heard by the ear alone, for it involves the heart center, just as it cannot be uttered by the mouth alone, for it also involves the mind.

The *mantra* releases its true power only for the initiated, that is, for those who have gone through a particular kind of training connected with its meaning and use. Just as a chemical formula empowers those acquainted with the laws of its application, similarly a *mantra* gives true power only to those who are aware of its inner significance, who know its methods of operation and who have awakened its psychophysical potentiality to call up "dormant forces within us through which we are capable of directing our destiny and influencing our surroundings." In a useful metaphor, a *mantra* has been compared to a magnifying glass. It is a means of *concentrating already existing forces* just as a magnifying glass, containing no innate power of its own, is able to concentrate the sun's rays and transform their warmth into heat and fire, a simple "trick" which would appear altogether mysterious, magical, even godlike to primitives.

Another "skillful means" employed in Northern Buddhism (particularly in Tibet, Japan and, in the past, China) as a support for meditative practice is the mandala, or sacred diagram. *Mandala* is another Asian word now found in common Western parlance, due in part to the pioneer discoveries of analytical psychologists like Dr. Carl Jung, who found mandala-like images arising from the troubled depths of the psyches of patients totally unfamiliar with Asian metaphysics or art. This discovery led Jung to his belief in a worldwide universality of certain symbols, the presence of "archetypes" in a "collective unconscious."

Dr. Jung's own description of a mandala is simple and comprehensive.)

The Sanskrit word *mandala* means "circle" in the ordinary sense of the word. In the sphere of religious practices and in psychology it denotes circular images, which are drawn, painted, modelled, or danced. Plastic structures of this kind are to be found, for instance, in Tibetan Buddhism, and as dance figures these circular patterns occur also in Dervish monasteries. As psychological phenomena they appear spontaneously in dreams, in certain states of conflict, and in cases of schizophrenia. Very frequently they contain a quaternity or a multiple of four, in the forms of a cross, a star, a square, an octagon, etc. In alchemy we encounter this motif in the *quadratura circuli*.*

* See *Mandala Symbolism*, C. G. Jung, Bollingen Series, Princeton, 1972.

The idea of the presence of "universal archetypes" in man's unconscious mind—once a subject of hot debate—is now widely accepted. In *The Theory and Practice of the Mandala*, Dr. Giuseppe Tucci, the great archaeologist and Tibetologist, has said of the archetypes: "They are innate in the soul of man . . . and therefore reappear in different lands and at different epochs, but with a similar aspect whenever man seeks to reconstruct that unity which the predominance of one or another of the features of his character has broken down or threatens to demolish." In other words, West as well as East, the psychic constructs called mandala are designed to correct imbalance; they are used to conquer disequilibrium in one's own nature. The difference is that Asians long ago formalized them, whereas in the West we still seem for the most part to be personally drawing them forth from the depths of a troubled psyche during a healing process.

It is not our purpose here to establish comparisons among the types of mandala and ways in which they are used. The names of Dr. Jung and Dr. Tucci have been introduced merely to indicate how related to modern thinking certain Asian psychological practices prove to be. There is something reassuring, in a time of Babel, to be presented with a concept of universal archetypes expressing themselves in symbols from many cultures; symbols intrinsically related to one another and thus perhaps in turn to a broader consciousness shared by all men.

In a contemporary book titled simply *Mandala*, José and Miriam Argüelles find an expression of "sacred consciousness" in a wide variety of man-made mandala-like constructs ranging from Navaho sand paintings to the plan of Stonehenge, and from Gothic rose windows to the Palenque Stone of the Incas. They also find this same consciousness on another scale altogether, in the human eye or seeds from plants and other natural forms. To these authors, all mandala—man-made or natural—conform to the Hermetic statement: "God is an intelligent sphere whose center is everywhere and whose circumference is nowhere."

One of the conclusions of the Argüelleses is that if man could only *see* clearly as true *seers* have always seen, there would be no need for mandala "because experience would be apprehended as an organic whole, continually proceeding from and returning to the one source—the center of being." They postulate that the ancient seers had a direct perception of reality and they wonder whether this penetration into Isness was simply due to the cultural situation of the time, i.e., man's conscious mind in the past was less encumbered with perceptual data than it is today. (This assumption would deductively account for the appearance of mandala in modern man's *un*conscious.) Whether the formalized sacred mandala of the past, as created by man from many cultures, is attributable to some source of higher teaching now lost to us or whether they merely reflect freedom from today's manifold conflicting and concealing perceptions, they are undeniably tools by which it is possible to reorient one's self to the total universe. This is clearly the aim of Tibet's sacred formalizations.

If *mantra* is, as we have said earlier, a means of concentrating already existing forces, and mandala is a tool by which it is possible to reorient one's self to the total universe, then visualization, a characteristic form of Tibetan meditation, is the method through which the *mantra* and mandala are activated and their innate powers made real by the aspirant. After having become familiar with the various other modes or forms of Buddhist meditation—*samatha, vipassana,* and general mindfulness exercises (Theravadin practices which are used by both Mahayana and Tantrayana practitioners and of which many of their own meditation methods are further elaborations)—the novice has a strong foundation to begin the long and arduous practice of visualization. He works with a personal guru who teaches him specific visualizations

*Northern Buddhism uses mandalas, or sacred diagrams, as a supportive device in meditative practice. Under the guidance of accredited teachers, these exactly designed diagrammatic paintings are tools by which it is possible to orient oneself to the total universe. Nineteenth century, Tibetan.*

Lha-mo. *The forceful, hyperenergetic nature of so much of Northern Buddhism's religious art appears almost to reflect the qualities of physical existence in this fiercely challenging mountain environment. It should be remembered that seemingly fearsome Buddhist deities play subtle roles in Tantric self-exploration.*

designed to suit his own nature and his degree of personal understanding until slowly over the course of years, with daily application and continued tutoring from the guru, the desired results are obtained.

As John Blofeld has said: ". . . visualization is a yoga of the mind. Its purpose is to gain control of the mind, become skilled in creating mental constructions, make contact with powerful forces (themselves the projections of mind) and achieve higher states of consciousness in which . . . the non-dual nature of reality is transformed from intellectual concepts into experiential consciousness—non-duality is no longer just believed but felt."

Transformation is the key word in the practice of visualization. The novice, through the course of intensive training, learns to identify himself with, and in essence become, a particular "deity," which is to say a personified mind force, or power of the mind, within the enormous pantheon of deities belonging to the Tibetan tradition. Through the use of *mudras* (specific gestures and postures he assumes while practicing), along with mantras and mandalas, the aspirant activates body, speech and mind in becoming wholly concentrated and absorbed in his meditation. While within this state of rapt absorption he creates a mental vision of the deity with whom he seeks union. Assuming the qualities and potentialities of this deity, he makes them manifest and is transformed.

We must remember that for the Vajrayana adept the internal and the external world are not separate. Therefore, the question of the validity or "reality" of the mentally constructed deity is not present. What is proved in the process of visualization practice is that the mind is the preeminent power in the creation of reality, that through the control of our own thoughts we can create worlds as real as, if not more so than, the "world" which is commonly accepted as the end-all and be-all of daily existence. One might say that the practitioner is becoming thoroughly familiar with the warp and woof of the "cloth" of life. He is learning how this cloth or this life is continually being created by the weaving of threads on the loom of our mind, how, through this very experience, he himself has been created and how he can re-create himself. Having transformed his own personality through this hard-won knowledge, he is then able to help others to achieve the same end. This is in effect the fulfillment of the *Bodhisattva* vow.

Under the influence of the peaceful, compassionate and reasonable faith of Buddhism, reaching Tibet as early as the seventh and eighth centuries, Tibetan rulers brought about changes in their country's culture comparable to those wrought by monarchs like Ashoka in India and Mongkut in Siam. King Songsten Gampo, who came to the Tibetan throne in A.D. 642, had two devout Buddhist queens, one a royal princess from Nepal, the other the daughter of the Chinese Emperor. Under their enlightened influence the King instituted many social reforms. He encouraged agriculture, crafts and all the arts and, most important, the manufacture of paper and ink for books. In succeeding generations other Tibetan rulers followed Songsten Gampo's notable example. This early, Buddhism-influenced monarchical lineage is said to have peaked in the time of Tretsong Detsan, who came to the throne in A.D. 765 and was instrumental in bringing to Tibet many great Buddhist teachers from such noted centers of learning as the Indian universities of Nalanda and Vikramasala, both destined to be tragically destroyed by fanatic Islamic invaders of the subcontinent. It was also in the period of Tretsong Detsan's rulership that a royal decree was issued which is said to have first effectively joined the teaching of Hinayana, Mahayana and Tantrayana as one finds them today in contemporary Tibetan teaching.

Under still another king, Repachen, who held the throne from A.D. 817 to 836, a notable council was convened in Tibet to determine ways to further the propagation of Buddhism. At this council the rough Tibetan language, then already undergoing amplification and polishing, was thoroughly revised. New words were coined, philosophical terms were accurately defined, and rules were laid down for the writing and translating of *sutras*. As a result of this council, the Buddhist scriptures in foreign tongues brought into Tibet were not only scrupulously translated but carefully preserved, along with a wide range of noncanonical literature, including works on such subjects as medicine and poetry.

There exists today a very large body of canonical scriptures in Tibet, including the famous Kangyur and Tangyur. The former is made up of the Buddha's teachings as translated from the Sanskrit. It is published in two editions, one of 104 and one of 108 volumes, and is considered the most important and sacred of the many Tibetan religious writings. The Tangyur is a collection of commentaries on the *sutras*, written by noted Indian and Tibetan scholars of the past.

In the eleventh century, after a period of shifting political power and patronage, a number of exceptional spiritual guides came to the fore, some from Indian centers, some born in Tibet. Among these teachers one can mention only a few: Atisha, Marpa, Naropa and Milarepa. The most venerated of all Tibetan teachers was Padmasambhava, the "Precious Guru," who came from India in the eighth century and founded what is sometimes known as the Old Tantric or Old Translation School. Throughout its long history, Tibetan Buddhist teachings have ranged from the most simple and fundamental instruction to the most exacting Tantric practices, the latter in particular under the guidance of the transplanted Indian pundit Naropa, whom one finds so often cited in Tibetan literature.

Few countries have a more richly varied and colorful history than Tibet, and when the names and chronicles of those who helped form its unusual sociological and religious structures have become familiar to non-Tibetans, it seems safe to say that accounts of its past will be read with worldwide interest. It also seems quite safe to prophesy that Tibetan Buddhism, now putting down strong roots in the West, is well on its way to becoming a vital living tradition in the alien lands to which it has so unexpectedly journeyed.

The first visit to America in the autumn of 1979 by His Holiness, the Dalai Lama, served with surprising immediacy to break down

*One of the world's most spectacular examples of sacred architecture is the Potala (sometimes called the "Buddhist Vatican") in Lhasa, Tibet—the former residence of the now-exiled Dalai Lama, and a vast treasure house of literature and art from the entire Buddhist world. Seventeenth century.*

any sense of insuperable cultural differences which might have been assumed to exist between countries as unlike one another as America and Tibet.

Traveling as a private citizen, conspicuously unprotected by official security of any kind and with only the most modest of entourages, this dignified, warm and intelligent potentate in his simple red garments impressed all who saw him by his humanness, his humor, his quick intelligence, his amazing interest in, and grasp of, the achievements of modern science and the weighty problems of the modern world. Because of the simplicity of his dress and bearing, the strongest first impression he made was not

that of being different but of being like, even though his direct unmannered presence suggested some interior strength, unfamiliar to most of us, in which he was firmly rooted.

His American trip (which coincided roughly with that of Pope John Paul II) was characterized by an almost complete absence of fanfare and pomp. The quiet manner of the Dalai Lama's travel astonished all Westerners acquainted with his still-accepted status among his own people as a veritable "god king," the spiritual and temporal head of a beautiful legendary land whose manifold natural resources and strategic geographic location have made it a recent target of exploitative foreign aggression. Despite the notable simplicity and naturalness of his behavior, however, the Dalai Lama by no means gave the impression of a ruler stripped of all power and influence; instead, he seemed quite clearly to be drawing on much more subtle sources of power than those embodied in worldly titles. Although newspaper accounts wherever he traveled reminded readers of his own personal ordeals—his flight from Tibet, his exile in India—the Dalai Lama himself did not dwell on these facts of his recent life even when attending gatherings organized to raise funds for less fortunate Tibetan exiles. The word "compassion" was often on his lips but used in a worldwide context, and it was perhaps this frequently used word, along with his own unaffected simple humanness, which drew people to him, giving them a sense of his own sharing of mankind's present, almost universal experience of suffering, deprivation and loss. It was easy to comprehend how faithful Tibetans could see him as the incarnation of the great *Bodhisattva* Avalokiteshvara.

# Zen
# Buddhism

Zen (Ch'an) is a Chinese-Japanese branch of Mahayana Buddhism widely known in the West today by its brief three-letter Japanese designation. Legend attributes the origin of Zen's special way of teaching to Bodhidharma, a far-wandering iconoclastic and perhaps apocryphal Buddhist master from India who declared in a sixth-century interview with a Chinese emperor that Buddhism's basic tenets lay outside the scriptures; its teachings were directly transmitted from mind to mind and were in no way dependent on explanation in words. Bodhidharma's concise, somewhat cheeky exchange with Emperor Wu set the style for Zen's subsequent unorthodox approach to religious instruction and experience. Freed from attachment to specific sacred literature and thus able to make use of any written material that seemed pertinent to its teaching, Zen ironically has come to rival, if not outstrip, most other branches of Buddhism in the multiplicity of writings about it or central to it. This irony is particularly evident today, when Zen has become the target of so much miscellaneous interpretive literature that a large lay public is convinced it knows all about the subject, or at least enough to have opinions on its methods, aims and values. A quick glance at the Zen shelves in a well-stocked bookstore reveals something of the range of Zen's effect on the modern mind: *Zen and the Art of Motorcycle Maintenance, Zen in the Art of Helping, The Zen of Seeing, Zen in the Art of J. D. Salinger, Zen and the Birds of Appetite, Zen and Creative Management*—the list is long and singularly varied.

Without passing judgment on any of the books listed here, one must admit that their very numbers plus all the new translations of scriptures and commentaries do weigh heavily against the impulse to embark yet again on a brief general description of Zen's past and present history and its approach to "practice." There was, however, no possible way to omit Zen from these pages, since it has become one of the most influential of the several Asian philosophies which have made successful incursions into the modern West, and in spite of the widespread attention it has received in recent years, it seems clear that there do remain many interested Westerners who still feel uninformed and would like to understand better a Buddhist way which they find oddly appealing though often puzzling.

Although Zen as a school developed some one thousand years after the death of the historic Indian Buddha, its particular form of Buddhism is considered to be a return to the Buddha's emphasis on meditation and his long sitting under the Bo Tree preceding his Enlightenment. Zen is an inevitable development from that challenging statement made by Buddhism's founder, frequently referred to in these pages, "Look within, *thou* art the Buddha," and the Great Teacher's deathbed exhortation to his disciples, that all seekers of the way *must make the effort themselves*. Personal effort is the very foundation and meaning of all practice, for only through disciplined individual exertion can one attain what is known in Zen as *kensho*, or *satori*, the opening into the world of enlightenment.

Zen's unflagging insistence on finding out for oneself, in accordance with the Buddha's early teachings on self-reliance, obviously appeals to many modern people who find it difficult to accept specific fixed dogma or sacrosanct religious authority in a world now in the midst of scientific and philosophic flux. As a consequence, in recent years Zen has been brought to the West not only by Japanese *roshis* (masters) but also by Western-born teachers, usually after periods of training in Japanese temples or monasteries. Through body-mind techniques of quiet sitting and also through the challenge of a certain kind of dynamic conundrum known as the *koan*, Zen instruction aims to curb the aggressive power of the ego, to make possible, in a revelation beyond the reach of words, a vivid awareness of the universe as an indissoluble unity, a totality of which man is an integral part—but not its arbitrary master!

The very heart of Zen practice lies in *zazen*, or sitting meditation done at specific times daily, with longer and more intensive periods on occasions of *sesshin*, in which concentrated "sitting" may endure for as long as a week. *Zazen* is a formalized procedure which consists of active meditation interspersed with the chanting of *sutras*. In this daily Zen chanting the *sutra* known as the *Prajna Paramita* is always included. The actual sitting itself is preceded by prescribed use of bells, wooden clappers and the exchange of formal bows. Practitioners sit facing a wall or the center of the *zendo*, depending on the tradition of the specific sect to which the group belongs or the preference of the presiding Zen *roshi*. The usual *zazen* posture is the full lotus or half-lotus cross-legged sitting position on a specific type of round cushion. The position of the hands is strictly specified: they are held in front of the abdomen, the back of the left in the palm of the right, the thumbs lightly touching. The eyes are not closed, although the gaze is directed downward and is fixed a little in advance of the sitter. *Zazen* is terminated by the sound of wooden clappers, the ringing of a bell three times and the chanting of the Four Great Vows. Periods of formal sitting may be interspersed by walking meditation, known as *kinhin*. This is essentially a method for giving the body relief from the prolonged sitting posture, but it serves also as a way of practicing concentration, whether during a slow circling of the *zendo* or in a brisk walk outside.

Most Western Zenists adhere to traditional forms of practice and ceremony, except in the case of marriages and funerals, when it is the custom for each *roshi* to create his own services within the basic form handed down through his specific lineage.

Zen's emphasis on direct perception of truth or reality has been described in modern psychological terms as a way of connecting with the deep unconscious to the end that one becomes what one truly is: as the tree grows, the bird flies, the cloud forms. Here, however, one must warn against attempting to equate Zen terms (or, for that matter, general Buddhist terms) with the Western psychological vocabulary. They do not fit one another with any true exactitude. As an instance, Zen's concept of "Emptiness" or the "Void" could perhaps be considered an approximation of Carl Jung's "collective unconscious" only if one thinks of them both in terms of D. T. Suzuki's definition as "the source of infinite possibilities." These words might also be said to relate to the Zen term "no-mind," which implies freedom from the tyranny of conceptual thought and reliance on other bodily energies and abilities, as so ably described in the widely read classic *Zen in the Art of Archery* by Eugen Herrigel. This is an account of a Westerner's struggles with a bow and arrow and his eventual achievement in learning to relax with *awareness* and let "it" shoot for him.

Zen holds that the so-called rational mind is incapable of solving an individual's deepest problem: his meaning to himself and to life. There is no way, in the Zen view, that conclusive answers to existential questions can be found by discussion, dialectic, or even ordinary thought. Final awareness, lasting freedom, and true psychological equilibrium come only when the deepest intuitional faculties of the human being have been tapped. It follows that, in Zen, reason is never permitted the unquestioned place of rulership it has occupied for centuries in Western philosophy. Zen holds that the reasoning process's function is separation, discrimination and the division of "this" from "that," thus making it impossible ever to see life's *wholeness* and oneself in relation to it. In Zen, since All-is-One, knowledge of one's own true nature predicates knowledge of all nature, or the universe itself.

As the pattern of Zen's unorthodox approach to religious instruction—especially in its traditional use of sharp and pithy exchanges between master and pupil—was so clearly foreshadowed in Bodhidharma's precedent-shattering interview with the Emperor Wu in sixth-century China, the full legend, no matter how often repeated, properly belongs at the beginning of any general account of Zen Buddhism.

At the time of Bodhidharma's arrival in China from India, so we are told, the Emperor Wu-ti, in residence at Nanking, was already a devout Buddhist. Buddhism had been in China since A.D. 61, and had experienced the usual fluctuations in prestige and popularity common to all transplanted faiths—for that matter, to indigenous ones as well. The Emperor, once an ardent Confucianist, had become an equally ardent Buddhist whose behavior subsequent to his conversion could be compared to that of the Indian Emperor Ashoka. He had forbidden cruelty to animals, sought to abolish capital punishment, was responsible for the translation of many Sanskrit manuscripts and, in person, frequently expounded Buddhist scriptures to his subjects. Like Mongkut, the famous nineteenth-century King of Siam, he had lived for a time as a Buddhist monk, although not for as extended a period and never as an abbot.

When Emperor Wu summoned Bodhidharma, the noted Indian Buddhist teacher, to the Nanking court for a private audience it was, as the legend relates, quite natural for him to speak of the temples he had built in the Buddha's name, the many sacred scriptures he had had translated and copied, the special privileges he had granted Buddhist monks and nuns. Perhaps because this recital of his munificence seemed to arouse very little enthusiastic response from his noted visitor, the Emperor ventured to inquire what degree of "merit" all this had earned him. Without a moment's hesitation, Bodhidharma replied bluntly, "No merit whatsoever!" The astonished Emperor next inquired which among the holy teachings of Buddhism was the most important, or, in other words, what did the learned sage consider the First Principle of Buddhism. "Vast Emptiness and nothing holy," replied Bodhidharma. Chagrined, nettled, but still curious, His Majesty then inquired, "Who are you who thus replies to me?" Bodhidharma's answer was: "I do not know." With that he took himself off, to cross the mighty

Yang-tze River, symbolically traveling upright on a floating reed bound for a distant cave to undertake a nine-year stint of sitting meditation, which was subsequently to become known as *zazen*.

This account of Bodhidharma's conversation with the Chinese Emperor is not meant to suggest that Zen's First Patriarch was an ill-mannered lout who indulged in willful mystification. There was serious intention behind each of his replies—perhaps somewhat dramatically truncated during many centuries of word-of-mouth recounting. Most important, the story illustrates Zen's antipathy to lengthy verbalism. Further, in denying the possibility of merit or measurable rewards for worldly deeds, Bodhidharma was rejecting the "doctrine of works" and suggesting—without directly saying so—that overattention to forms and rituals, monuments, images and scholarly scriptures would never bring liberation. Disciplined personal meditation, *zazen*, as practiced by the historic Buddha, both before and *after* his Enlightenment, is in Zen the one and only way to the goal of self-knowledge and thus to the knowledge of the world "as it is."

As for the answer that "Vast Emptiness" was Buddhism's First Principle, Bodhidharma was here stressing the doctrine of the nondualistic eternal Void, that fullness without boundaries from which all life emerges and which must be personally experienced in order to grasp life's true meaning and significance. Emptiness is a positive rather than a negative concept. The early stages of Zen training stress "Empty the Mind." Sometimes the aspirant is advised to "Take as thought the thought of No-thought." Or it may be suggested that he not seek so hard after the "truth," but simply begin by "ceasing to cherish opinions."

To understand Bodhidharma's reply to the Emperor about his identity, it is necessary to tread warily in the tricky fields of explanation. It might be said that to avoid mouthing a lot of high-sounding words the First Patriarch of Zen by answering "I do not know" was simply suggesting that in the vast Oneness of the Universe there is truly no-self (*anatman*), a basic Buddhist concept. Although one is warned that this enigmatic reply "was a plain fact stated in plain language," it is worth noting that solving the meaning of Bodhidharma's third response to the Emperor is one of the so-called *koans*, those irrational "riddles" which play such a significant role in certain forms of Zen training.

Bodhidharma's independent style has remained Zen's style down the centuries. It seems both to exasperate and to attract Western people. Whatever the reaction to its teaching methods, Zen calmly goes its ancient Bodhidharma way, a way that reflects the essential attitude of the historic Indian Buddha, who, although he handled his ripostes differently, was equally unwilling to engage in long-drawn-out discussions on subjects that could not, by their very nature, ever lend themselves to specific solution in words. It will be remembered that when questioned about life's meaning, about "the reality of the self," about the "origins of the universe," the Buddha maintained a "noble silence." Silence can also be Zen's way in the face of any questions considered irrelevant to the personal effort involved in attaining spiritual freedom, effort which demands much more than a mere exercise of the forebrain or one's wits. Intellectual curiosity, so Zen would say, is all very well in itself, but it bears no promise of final release from the pressures and problems created by the restless, ever unsatisfied human ego. The most brilliant verbalism, no matter how seemingly irrefutable, cannot answer the fundamental human questions—Who? What? Why? Reason, it is all too plain, can be used to refute itself; one theory simply leads to another, on and on without end. Reality cannot be reached by way of argument or any so-called facts. To reiterate: there is only one course to pursue, and that is regular disciplined "sitting practice," or *zazen*, which the West calls "meditation," although the terms are not synonymous.

Four famous and often-quoted lines attributed to Bodhidharma succinctly express the classic Zen viewpoint:

> A special tradition outside the scriptures,
> No dependence on words,
> A direct pointing at man,
> Seeing into one's own nature and the attainment of wisdom.

The key phrase here is "seeing into one's own nature." D. T. Suzuki, the Japanese scholar who introduced Zen to the West in his many interpretive volumes of Zen studies, considered these five words to be "the most significant ever uttered in the development of Zen."

Although some thirteen centuries have passed since Bodhidharma's utterance, it is this phrase and others like it that have turned many Western psychologists—including among others Carl Jung, Erich Fromm, Hubert Benoit and Karen Horney—to an interest in Zen approaches to self-realization. Existentialists also, of the stature of Martin Heidegger, have claimed to find in ancient Zen some of the very ideas they have been developing on their own in the present century. As already suggested, one must be very wary of laying too much weight on psychological interpretations or comparisons. Zen's methodology is unique, representing in its flowering a blend of ancient Indian mysticism, influenced during its passage through China by the humanist and pragmatic qualities of Confucianism as well as by the quietism and Nature-love of the Taoists—all of these contributory elements sieved through the special mesh of the Japanese national character. This book concerns itself chiefly with Japanese Zen. It should be recognized, however, that Zen's indebtedness to Chinese Ch'an can hardly be overestimated. Further on, we will speak of the specific manner in which Ch'an traveled from China to Japan.

In his monumental history of Japanese Buddhism, Sir Charles Eliot remarks that Buddhism's entry into Japan, by way of China and Korea in the sixth century, could hardly be described as "glorious." In fact, it got its first toehold through claims put forth by ambitious political Buddhists that a certain Buddha image had power to arrest a plague then sweeping the country. What was essentially a power struggle between rival clans and the rival claims of ancient Shintoism and of various orders of newly transplanted Buddhism was waged back and forth with the usual attendant assassinations and martyrdoms common to religious history everywhere. This sorry part of early Buddhist annals in Japan should not, however, warns Eliot, blind us to the fact that Buddhism came to Japan as the very epitome of the highest Indian and Chinese civilization and was destined to bring about a moral and intellectual revolution in what was then, outside certain small aristocratic circles, a barbarous country.

During Japan's internal strife in the sixth century, Soga Yumako, a member of one of the powerful contending clans, became in effect the ruler of Japan and, for political reasons, one of Buddhism's strong supporters. After much unsavory intrigue, this high-born but ruthless opportunist permitted the designation of his niece, Suiko, as official Empress, probably in the hope of sidestepping the dire consequences of his deserved unpopularity.

In reading about the Empress Suiko, we cannot but be reminded of the two Tibetan queens, one from China, the other from Nepal, who influenced the Tibetan monarch Songsten Gampo to encourage and promote Buddhism. Suiko ruled Japan, in name at least, for twenty-five years, during which she encouraged Buddhism by lending it her royal patronage and performing many meritorious activities on its behalf.

This new faith which had recently reached Japan by way of China and Korea found its outstanding patron and chief supporter, however, in Shotoku Taishi (A.D. 574–622), a Prince Imperial whom the Empress had named Regent. An altogether admirable personage, Shotoku Taishi made himself the most influential and important figure of his era in Japan. Like Ashoka in India, Wu-ti in China, Mongkut in Siam, Shotoku lived the life of a fervent Buddhist, dedicated not only to religion but to scholarship, humanitarianism and aesthetics. He promoted the building of the great temple complex at Horyuji, destined to become a famed museum and storehouse for some of Japan's most impressive religious art. (A designated National Treasure, the Horyuji was tragically damaged by fire in 1949.)

In his person and behavior, Shotoku exemplified the best aspects of a faith which, in spite of the ignoble political uses to which it was sometimes put, did produce seeds of moral, intellectual and aesthetic progress wherever it traveled. Prince Shotoku earnestly attempted to incorporate Buddhism's moral teachings into his country's political and social life.

Some of this noble Prince's aims and achievements have been described by Yūhō Yokoi in his book *Zen Master Dōgen:*

One of Prince Shotoku's first acts upon assuming power was to proclaim Buddhism the state religion. He called for the foundation of a grand Buddhist institution composed of a temple, an asylum, a hospital, and a dispensary. In 604 he promulgated what is known as the first Japanese constitution (the content of which consisted of moral instructions), in which he stated that the rulership of a single monarch implied the equality of all people, just as faith in the unique personality of the Buddha as savior of all mankind presupposed the intrinsic value and destiny of every individual who was in communion with him. The high aims of the prince can be seen in the opening statements of his constitution's first article: "Harmony is to be valued, and discord is to be deprecated. . . . All men are influenced by partisanship, and there are few who have wide vision."

In the second article, the prince enunciated his vision of spiritual harmony based on Buddhism: "Simply revere the Three Treasures. The Three Treasures are the Buddha, the Law, and the Buddhist community [*Sangha*], the final resort of all beings and the supreme object of faith for all peoples. Should any age or any people fail to revere this truth? There are few men who are utterly vicious. Everyone will realize it if duly instructed. Can any wickedness be corrected without having resort to the Three Treasures?"

Shotoku recognized in Buddhism an effective instrument for promoting national unity due to the universality of its concepts, which were in marked contrast to those of Japan's indigenous original faith, which had always been associated with clan rivalries and local powers and gods. This ancient amorphous religion had remained nameless until after the arrival of Buddhism, when it acquired the designation of Shintoism, meaning the Way of the Gods, to distinguish it from the Way of Buddha, or Buddha *Dharma*. Through the centuries the two ways have coexisted in relative harmony to a degree that makes it possible for a modern Japanese to claim without apparent conflict both Shinto and Buddhist allegiance.

Interestingly enough, Shinto from very early days possessed a number of qualities that resemble Zen, in particular what Sir Charles Eliot has called "earth-relatedness" and, even more significant, a sophisticated sense of the aesthetic rightness of simple natural forms. These latter characteristics are exemplified perhaps most strongly in the famous Shinto shrine at Ise. This treasured shrine building, although accurately described as "prehistoric," has been ritualistically rebuilt in its entirety every two decades, thus preserving it for more than two thousand years as a superb example of ancient Japanese taste. In certain respects the Ise shrine can be seen as a prototype of the Japanese Zen temple, set as it is in a graveled garden, with its thatched roof, its encircling veranda, its general lack of ostentation, even in its absence of "color" (in the Western sense), depending only on weathered woods to provide the variety of monochromatic tones which distinguish it.

In evaluating the tremendous influence of China on Japan from the dynasties of T'ang through the Northern and Southern Sung to Yuan, roughly a period of four centuries, one should be careful not to underestimate the part played by the Japanese in civilizing themselves. Despite the general barbarism and ignorance of the Japanese populace during this period, there did exist among the elite not only a keen appreciation of the advanced civilization of China but, more than this, the ability to contribute some of their own refinements to these importations. The Japanese brought more than exceptional eagerness to acquiring the subtleties of Chinese civilization; they brought also certain inherent characteristics which enabled them in time to refine and develop a transplanted aesthetic into their own unique expression.

A further brief digression on the Japanese aesthetic sense in relation to their various borrowings and assimilations is not out of place here, for the interaction of Buddhist teachings with Japanese culture is a vital part of Buddhism's social history in Japan. (This is particularly true of Zen, as we shall see.) Exquisite refinements were common to the upper classes in Japan as early as the Heian era (794–1185). A style of living developed among the aristocracy which equaled if it did not surpass the elegant sensibilities of the Chinese elite. This fascinating interlude in Japan's history is known to the West chiefly through two famous literary classics, both written by women: *The Tale of Genji* and *The Pillow Book of Lady*

*Sei Shonogen.*\* They tell us in detail about the tastes and customs of an exalted circle of aristocrats who were also the intellectuals of the day. These fortune-favored people communicated with one another exclusively through mannered expressions in art, poetry, letters, flowers, scents and details of dress. This living aesthetic of the Heian era, today almost inconceivable in its subtlety, reached such an extreme stage of refinement that the use of an unacceptable color in the barely visible edging of a kimono sleeve could fatefully affect one's destiny.

Among these Heian aristocrats, whose preciosity and rigidly prescribed formal conduct were reinforced by an overrefined and effete Buddhism, the highest of the arts was considered "brushwork"—that is, calligraphy. Through an individual's use of the brush, in the hastiest sketch or briefest verse, or even the most secret billet-doux, it was deemed possible to judge the writer's character, sensitivity and exact degree of cultivation. This so painstakingly acquired calligraphy was also expected to convey "disciplined spontaneity," and in doing so presaged the kind of calligraphy and painting soon to appear under the aegis of Zen, which was destined to bring to the Japanese an entirely fresh and distinctive set of values and a new and original critical vocabulary.

It was in the twelfth and thirteenth centuries, while China, although beset with troubles, was at its greatest intellectual and artistic heights—the eras of Northern Sung (960–1127) and Southern Sung (1127–1279)—that Japanese priests and scholars had begun in significant numbers to travel to the Middle Kingdom and experience at first hand the refinements and creativity of the Chinese. The Japanese, always eager and gifted learners once their interest is engaged, brought back from their travels reports of the high degree of civilization achieved by their powerful neighbors, and, more important, tangible proof in works of art and literature. These, as a matter of fact, they had already been quietly importing

* *The Tale of Genji*, Murasaki Shikibu, tr. Arthur Waley, Houghton Mifflin & Company, New York, 1935. *The Pillow Book of Lady Sei Shonogen*, tr. Ivan Morris, Penguin, New York, 1971. See also *The World of the Shining Prince*, Ivan Morris, Alfred A. Knopf, New York, 1964, and *The Vermillion Bridge*, Shelley Mydans, Doubleday, New York, 1980.

for some time, along with ways of teaching and practicing Buddhism which, though centuries old in other parts of Asia, had not yet assumed an ascendant role in Japan. It is no exaggeration to say that when Ch'an Buddhism, that special flowering of certain sensitivities of the Chinese nature, was eventually taken over by the Japanese (to become Zen) it infiltrated the entire structure of Japanese life from popular education in village temple schools to what today we would call the civil service, commerce, the military, statesmanship and, above all, the arts—a striking tribute to the versatility and dynamism of the Japanese *Sangha*. Most important, Zen temples became in effect schools of art, where artists of the first rank and enduring fame were trained, and in spite of Zen's rejection of formal dependence on scriptural authority, these temple sanctuaries also encouraged literature, notably poetry, "as a help and ornament of the religious life."

On entering Japan in the twelfth century, Zen had been taken up and encouraged by the samurai, the ruling military class of the period, who were drawn to Zen largely because of its emphasis on strict self-discipline and the overcoming of the fear of death. The outward effects of this exacting Zen training were dramatically illustrated by Japanese successes in resisting the destructive raids of the Mongols which had already so crippled and devastated China. The direct agent of Japan's miraculous escape from these nomadic raiders was a "Divine Wind," named, by a grateful emperor, *Kamikaze* (in actuality a very timely typhoon which effectively dispersed the Mongol fleet—not once but twice). But before these fortuitous circumstances of weather, the samurai, trained in new types of physical, and especially psychological, Zen disciplines, had been giving a very good account of themselves as warriors. Their gallant seven-week resistance, prior to the providential August hurricane, had in fact so brilliantly demonstrated the effectiveness of Zen training, not only in archery and swordsmanship but in inner control and absence of fear, that this new type of instruction was destined to become a part of Japanese martial tactics from then on. For a concise and clear account of this episode in Zen's infiltration of Japan, see Thomas Hoover's admirable *Zen Culture*.

❖

It was during the period of maximum Chinese influence on Japan and lively interchange between these two countries that two outstanding Japanese Zen Masters, Eisai and Dōgen, both trained in China, left their lasting imprint on Japanese Zen. Eisai (1141–1215) is credited with introducing the *koan* type of Zen training, known as Rinzai Zen. He is considered the founder of this branch of Zen in Japan. Dōgen (1200–1253), who brought home from his Chinese experiences the *zazen*-oriented type of Zen known as Soto, to which he made many valuable contributions, is considered the founder of this latter branch of Zen in Japan.

Although the main lines of both Rinzai and Soto descend from the so-called Sudden Enlightenment School of Hui Neng, the sixth Patriarch, and are based on *zazen* and *koan* study, their emphasis and style of teaching are different. In Rinzai, it is the teacher who tends to define the student-teacher relationship and the focus of the teaching; it is he who chooses the student's *koan* and directs his *zazen* practice. In Soto it is more the student's responsibility to define his relationship to the teacher and to create his own focus of practice. He chooses his *koan* and methods of breathing practice, suggests them to his teacher and thus initiates a ground for further relationship and work.

Because *zazen* is so primary to the practice of Zen in both schools, it seems wise to remind ourselves again that the familiar word "meditation," now in such current usage in the West, is not an adequate translation of "sitting practice," or *zazen*. Meditation implies to think or concentrate *on* something. *Zazen* means to *stop* thinking.

In his valuable *Three Pillars of Zen*, Philip Kapleau, an American-born *roshi*, translates *zazen* as "actualization of the Buddha nature: or one's own 'true nature.'" Another revered modern teacher, the late Shunryu Suzuki Roshi of the San Francisco Zen Center, stressed over and over again *not* the attainment of the Buddha nature, or any "goal" at all, but the necessity of remaining always a "beginner," which is to say to be able to repeat day after day, with an unfailingly fresh spirit, the essentials of practice; remaining open to whatever happens without dwelling on any possible benefits or results. This "remaining open beyond comparative thinking" may indeed be the "actualization of the Buddha Nature," says Shunryu Suzuki Roshi's "*Dharma* heir,"* Baker-roshi.

In *Zen Mind, Beginner's Mind*, Suzuki Roshi wrote: "If you think you will get something from practicing zazen, already you are involved in impure practice. . . . When you practice zazen, just practice zazen. If enlightenment comes, it just comes. We should not attach to the attainment. The true quality of zazen is always there, even if you are not aware of it. *Just do it.*"

This "just doing it" is one of the key precepts of Zen. By implication it involves a strict discipline far from easy for restless modern people to maintain. Dōgen, the thirteenth-century Master, declared, "The Way is attained through the body," because of "the unity of mind and body." Thus Zen expresses its centuries-old understanding that it is primarily through the physical practice of daily sitting that the mind can be taught to still itself, thereby making possible a self-discovery which is in reality an *uncovering* of something already present though unrecognized.

To quote from the Jesuit scholar-observer Heinrich Dumoulin in his *A History of Zen Buddhism*:

According to the Law of Buddha, body and mind are originally one; essence and form are not two. As essence and form are inseparable, so also are body and mind. When the body assumes the Buddha-form in taking the upright and motionless seated position, the mind is likewise in the dwelling [-place] of the Buddha. The crossed-legged sitting position, which permits the blood to circulate freely throughout the body, and stills the passions of anger, vexation, and selfishness while composing and emptying the mind, is not merely a prerequisite to the experience of enlightenment but in itself already constitutes enlightenment.

The word *koan* comes from the Chinese term *kung-an*. It originally meant a precedent-establishing formulation in the legal sense. In its Ch'an use, the *koan* embodied something of the exuberant spirit of enlightenment which characterized early Chinese Zen, a dynamic bursting of restrictive bonds, part of a spontaneous

* *Dharma* heir: One who, by transmission, inherits his teacher's position.

desire to be rid of lifeless religious dogma, to discard empty ritualized formulas and, instead, to be carried "by the storm of the spirit." When, in due course, this lively expression of a rejuvenated Buddhism began to fade in China, it was deemed expedient by certain members of the *Sangha* there to maintain some exact records of this vital experience to serve as example and illustration in less vigorous periods of Buddhist teaching and practice. Thus it came about, in spite of traditional emphasis on wordless instruction, that such a surprising number of aphorisms, sayings, verses, riddles from the past are to be found in the Zen branch of the many-branched Buddhist tree.

There is something about the seemingly irrational Lewis Carroll nonsense of a *koan*'s phrasing which has caught the imagination of many non-Orientals. Alan Watts once spoke of their "itchy fascination." They appear to be deliberately designed to throw the mind off its accustomed track, to detach it from its familiar habits of classification, division and comparison, plunging it instead directly into the vast sea of indescribable "Isness."

How can there be a mentally worked-out answer to such riddles as "What is the sound of one hand clapping?" or "What was your original face before your parents were born?" or "Has a dog Buddha Nature?" There cannot be. The Master Joshu gave as his reply to the latter question the single word *Mu*. *Mu* became and has remained a classic Zen conundrum.

*The Three Pillars of Zen* conveys a clear picture of the actual practice patterns that have survived around this most famous of all *koans*, considered unsurpassed for "breaking asunder the mind of ignorance and opening the eye of truth." By contrast to other *koans*—like those given above and similar ones which can act as "bait" to excite the imagination and arouse the discursive mind—the single word *Mu* offers absolutely no lure for either intellect or imagination. Therein lies its effectiveness. The novice who accepts the *koan Mu*, or has it assigned him, must focus on this single word unremittingly day and night with every ounce of energy he possesses. He is warned not to speculate, not to question, not to think, just to concentrate on *Mu* as a hen sits on an egg until it is hatched. When *Mu* is hatched, so to speak, the eternally restless activity of the mind has been brought to an abrupt halt and it is now possible for the aspirant, suddenly free of himself as observer and reactor, to experience the shock and recognition of his "true place" in the totality of the universe.

Whether emphasizing training in the *koan* practice, or *zazen*, the aim in Zen is to become wholly concentrated, not simply in thought or in the head, but *with one's entire being*. As a modern Zen Master has clearly stated: "The word Zen literally means unambivalent concentration or absorption."

In common with other Buddhist sects, but with special strictness and formality, Zen emphasizes the necessity of correct posture and breath-awareness in "sitting practice," for breath and posture relate to the vital center of the body—in Japanese, the *hara* or *tanden*—located between the navel and the pelvis. Although the formal cross-legged posture is the most recommended form of sitting, it is not necessary in Zen practice for those who cannot, for one physical reason or another, sustain it. There are only two absolutely essential physical rules by which every practitioner must abide: his back should be as straight as possible and his knees should never be higher than the hipbones because, if they are, strength from his *hara* cannot flow properly into the body.

The *hara* has special significance in the Zen view. A noted Western authority on the subject, Karlfried von Dürckheim, sees in it a "birthright" of man, lost during the evolution of his consciousness. It is one of life's "hidden treasures" which man, if he is to remain in proper balance, must somehow discover or rediscover. In this Western Zen philosopher's view, the true center of man's gravity lies in the *hara* (the belly, in our vocabulary), and it is the contemporary world's overemphasis on the head which is now doing man a dangerous disservice, since he tends to consider his intellect the complete arbiter of his fate and to ignore other and deeper sources of strength and creativity.

In truth, it is not mere overemphasis on the human mind as total master of man's destiny but our ignorance (until recent discoveries) of the brain's functioning which has helped lead us astray. We now know that the brain has two distinct halves or hemispheres which perform in different ways: the right hemisphere governs intuition and nonverbal perceptions, and the left governs our ability to analyze and to use logic. The Western world has long considered those functions recently identified with the left hemisphere of the brain to be the general overseer of man's fate. In the East, on the contrary, there has been a tendency to allow those identified with the right hemisphere to interpret the true nature of reality, its "operative functions," so to speak. (Here is the place where the irrational riddle of the Zen *koan* plays its part: denying solution in logic or conceptual analysis, stressing instead intuitive perception.)

In advocating the rediscovery of the *hara* and its proper use, von Dürckheim has said, "The descent into the center of the earth must always precede the ultimate ascent of the spirit." No matter how an individual in his everyday consciousness has estranged himself from the essential roots of his own nature, this innermost nature is still deeply connected with the true source of life. What will come, therefore, from prolonged practice of "sitting" day after day, in a given place and at a given time, is a slow process of getting in touch with the center of one's physical and mental being. A change—often perplexing to friends and family—occurs in the practitioner. He has begun to learn the difficult lesson of "letting go"—difficult because the modern world has taught him only how to cling, to keep, to preserve, to control, never how simply to give way, accept and trust. Yet this surrender by the tenacious ego is considered in Zen the only possible way to reach one's true being and become thereby rooted in the very ground of life itself.

Any assumption that Zen's stress on "sitting" implies passivity, inaction or withdrawal from the world is also wide of the mark. Through this very sitting activity—a very alive stillness—one's body and mind are refreshed and invigorated. A fuller awareness of our actual participation in all life develops and leads, naturally, to living more completely on every level.

The abbot of the Zen Center in San Francisco, Richard Baker, has written:

Zen meditation develops the clarity and calmness that allows one to meet and absorb the suffering and distractions of our life. The development of individuals who effectively know themselves as individuals and also as one with others is the main way that Buddhism tries to help people and society.

The central practice of Buddhism is mindfulness, which is the continual effort to at first note and later to just be one with the immediacy of one's situation; to break the adhesive of one's constant train of conceptual thought about past, present and future; and to bring oneself with clarity to the touch and consciousness of the present. The practice of mindfulness greatly deepens the power of concentration and the ability to stay with one's life situation.

These last words seem particularly pertinent and meaningful.

Many Japanese disciplines make specific use of the dynamic energy awakened through *zazen* and centered in the *hara*. Grounded in the Zen teaching of nonaggression and the practice of "letting go," the *hara*-related knowledge of the balance between the static and the dynamic, the in-breath and the out-breath, tension and relaxation, not only plays a significant part in such physical performances as judo (*jujitsu*), archery and ceremonial swordsmanship (*kendo*), but is also employed in the use of the brush in calligraphy and painting and in the spacing of movements in the tea ceremony and the ancient No drama.

In Zen monasteries, the work of the day is to be carried through with the same attention as that given the practice of *zazen* and *koan*. Work is accepted as a basic and integral part of human existence. In the midst of such ordinary activities as sweeping and cleaning, cooking and washing, even in administrative work, the individual should be able to find total concentration. No labor is considered beneath anyone's dignity; in every monastery, tasks are rotated as a part of the fixed monastic routine. One who has been in a position of power and influence, as for example, a manager or a treasurer, can find himself assigned to menial labor. A most respected modern Zen Master, the late Yasutani Roshi, even when he became a distinguished and famous abbot, continued doing self-assigned service in cleaning latrines.

The idea of service is central to the Zen way of life. Through disciplined meditation the interdependence of all beings and all things becomes clear, and from this understanding the ideal of service to others grows quite naturally.

It seems safe to assert that Zen more than any other religion has expressed its deepest essence in certain modes of life and forms of art which are inseparable from its philosophy. Although not always immediately perceptible, the links are unquestionably there. The No drama, the tea ceremony, the arranging of flowers, the use of *sumi* ink in painting, the plans of architecture and gardens, ceremonial swordsmanship, judo—all are enmeshed in a tacit Zen-ness. To treat any of these expressions of Zen philosophy in explicit terms is difficult, since it necessitates the use of a vocabulary foreign to Occidental criticism. Such terms as *wabi*,* *sabi*,* or even Emptiness, or Suchness, are apt to seem mere windy metaphysical abstractions to the average Westerner. To the Zen follower, on the contrary, because of his daily practice of *zazen* and his participation in Zen activities themselves, such terms are real and meaningful. Meditative practice has brought him the *personal discovery* of interior space and stillness, the essential connectedness of inner and outer, of rest in motion and motion in rest.

It was the deeply subjective nature of their *zazen* practice which made it possible for Zen artists to produce an art whose canons are quite unlike those of the West. Yet, in spite of this difference, Zen ink paintings (*sumi-e*) have the power to affect sensitive Western observers in ways which, although not easily analyzed, often serve as door openers into the subtleties of Zen culture. With a few powerful simple strokes, flowing spontaneity of line, delicate economy and precision in the use of ink, gifted Zen painters present

* See Glossary.

*Typical Zen monochrome landscape in which the aim is not realistic representation but the creation of an inward mood. Muromachi period. Bukūshō Shushō (active, late fifteenth–early sixteenth century). Hanging scroll; ink on paper.*

themes of water, rocks, trees, hermit huts, and misty mountains with such a quality of stillness, such a sense of "being" and "becoming" in the midst of utter repose, that the flurry of the onlooker's mind is singularly reduced as he looks at them. In the presence of these suggestive monochromes a feeling of concentration and peace arises. It is as though an invisible rhythm suggesting the indescribable yet perceptible energies of the Life Spirit in all its multiplicity and Oneness has been somehow realized on paper, or silk, through the simple medium of ink and a masterfully handled brush.

That the unique achievement of the greatest Zen art grew from the disciplined sitting practice of Zen monks is undeniable— a practice which inevitably led to an ever-deepening understanding of the meaning of "emptiness" in Buddhist thought. To Buddhists, as already noted, the quality of Voidness is not negative but positive. As expressed in the Heart Sutra, chanted daily in Zen monasteries, ". . . form does not differ from emptiness; emptiness does not differ from form. That which is form is emptiness; that which is emptiness, form."

It naturally follows from this profound perception, so contemporary in its equation of space and form, or matter, that Zen artists treat space not as something to be filled but as a quality existing in its own right. Henry P. Bowie, in his illuminating *On the Laws of Japanese Painting*, has described the Zen artist's spatial conception in these words: "Space was not to them a cubic volume that could be geometrically constructed, it was something illimitable and incalculable which might be, to some extent, suggested by the relation of forms and tonal values but which always extended beyond every material indication and carried a suggestion of the infinite."

This mysterious something—essentially inexpressible and indescribable, yet perceptible—which eternally abides in the midst of flux is given verbal embodiment in the Japanese word *yugen*: a term applicable not alone to painting but to other forms of Zen-influenced art, notably the No drama. Often referred to as a dance, although in our understanding of the term there seems to be barely any movement at all, the No drama is pervaded by a deeply suggestive unearthly silence which, as R. H. Blyth has pointed out, is "not immobility but a perfect balance of opposed forces." Here again one becomes aware of space and form as one. The initiated spectator at the No has learned to experience, for example—as the performer in front of him surely does—the *space* between the slow raising and lowering of a white tabi-clad foot when the principal actor, the *shite*, silently turns in one of his mythic movements, suspended somewhere outside time but within the immediate circumstances of the drama's tenuous plot.

❖

One of the most comprehensive treatments of Zen philosophy and its relationship to Zen arts is presented in Shin'Ichi Hisamatsu's *Zen and the Fine Arts*, a subject on which Dr. Hisamatsu is supremely qualified to speak, for he has long been a practicing lay Zen Master teaching advanced classes in Zen culture in his own country and at many Western universities, including Harvard. In this illuminating volume he writes from the position of actual personal experience through working with college students as well as advanced lay pupils dedicated to the practice and study of Zen and to keeping alive, in modern society, *Shincha-kai* or the "Spirit of the Way of Tea."

In his opening paragraphs, Dr. Hisamatsu stresses the working of the Zen "spirit," what he calls, specifically, Zen Activity. This activity may often seem to the kinetic Westerner to express no movement whatsoever, as when a sage sits in utter stillness under a tree or beside a waterfall; or when—again in the No drama—it is not the action on the stage which conveys the deepest meaning but rather the pauses and silences.

Zen "activity," in Hisamatsu's exposition, can be found in any number of ordinary objects or phenomena not usually recognized as belonging either to aesthetic or "religious" sensibilities: the sound of wind or water, a mossy stone, a weathered wooden pillar, an old gnarled tree, plum blossoms, certain kinds of movement, tea ceremony utensils—there are innumerable examples. In Zen the source, or wellspring, of the many everyday "realities" in the world of man and nature which though mundane are charged with significance could be said to be "space prior to form," a space filled with a potential, or "waiting" energy not yet visible although perceptible to those who have through proper concentration become acutely aware of its presence. This mysterious, commonly unrecognized all-prevailing dynamic is the "it" that finally released Eugen Herrigel's arrow when he was learning the art of archery (see p. 144).

Zen painting, or *sumi-e*, is notably free from attachment to, or overinvolvement in, what is being portrayed. Innumerable classic treatises may urge the artist to "become" what he paints, yet this is clearly not taken to imply some transcendental animism. It seems rather to suggest only a special Buddhist awareness of the profound relationship existing between the human being and all aspects of life around him.

Western analysts of Zen painting sometimes tell us that in these paintings "Nature is used as metaphor." This should not be taken in the sense of our "sermons in stones and books in running brooks." Zen teachers are disinclined to preach or sermonize; they are apt merely to comment or point out, as in the story of the master who remarked of a stone lying beside the temple gate, "All Buddhas of the Past, Present and Future reside therein." Or again, in the annals of Chinese Zen, the anecdote of the Ch'an Master Huen Sha, who was about to begin a talk to his pupils when a bird on a nearby bough burst into song. After listening raptly to the bird until it flew away, Huen Sha dutifully ascended his dais, only to descend again with the dry remark that the sermon for the day had already been given.

In Zen, the means and occasions of spiritual awakening are not dependent on either scriptural or supramundane experiences. When the mind is ripe, enlightenment may accompany the most commonplace event: the striking of a tile, the extinguishing of a candle or the quiet display of a flower in the hands of the teaching Buddha. The possibilities for such enlightenment, or at least the deepening of awareness, are the concern of Zen arts in general. They find their voice in the often seemingly incomprehensible master-pupil dialogues of Zen literature and above all in the stripped evocative poetry known as *haiku*. *Haiku* is a highly abbreviated verse of seventeen syllables dealing with the simplest of everyday observations. Its aim is to capture the sight, sound and feeling of a fleeting moment without any overlay of exposition, emotion or philosophizing. Even in translation these brief poems are able to convey a magical sense of "the intersection of the timeless and the ephemeral" to act as reminders of those many instances of fleeting insight which, though born of the simplest elements, often possess the power to linger in memory more vividly than dramatic events.

> The scent of plum blossoms
> on the mountain road—suddenly
> sunrise.

On a withered branch
a crow has settled—
autumn nightfall.

Sitting quietly doing nothing,
Spring comes.
Grass grows by itself.

Like the deliberately nonexplicit language of the No drama, these poems imply, in the Zen way, that the truth of experience cannot be conveyed in words, that, lying as it does beyond phraseology, it can only be suggested. Thomas Hoover tellingly makes this point in his *Zen Culture*, where he remarks that if Shakespeare's *King Lear* were written as a Japanese verse-drama, instead of chronicling Lear's own personal anguish it would speak in understated terms of the darkness of the heath on which he was wandering.

Comparisons of Western and Japanese poetry often prove useful, since they can illustrate certain basic differences which are clearly present even though poetic appreciation of Nature's endless "lessons" abounds in Western literature. R. H. Blyth's several volumes on *haiku*, and his *Zen in English Literature*, are mines of information in this particular field. The English poet Tennyson provided a singularly apt comparison in that once-familiar schoolroom classic, "Flower in the Crannied Wall." Not content merely to observe with pleasure a flower springing from a crack in a stone wall, the poet felt compelled to "pluck" it out of its cranny, "root and all, and all in all," thereby effectively ending its existence although enabling him, in the true Western analytical or scientific manner, to study the plant in his hand and muse on the mystery of its being. By contrast, there is an equally famous poem by the seventeenth-century Zen poet Basho, who, also musing on a humble weed, had only this to say:

When I look carefully
I see the *nazuna* blooming
Under the hedge!

The word "carefully" should be noted; it reflects the Zen concern with the development of unfailing awareness, the value of constant attention. Noteworthy also is the last word of this *haiku* as written in Japanese, *kano*. *Kano* is a particle which can be translated, as here, by an exclamation mark. Basho, the poet-observer, has employed the word to express his sense of the amazing wonder of a little flowering weed. Basho has looked; what is more, he has seen, he has responded with a deep sense of wonder but has been content to comment in the briefest terms and leave the little blossom just where he found it. This type of behavior brings to mind Emerson's admonitory lines:

> Hast thou named all the birds without a gun?
> Loved the wood-rose, and left it on its stalk?

It is worth remarking in this context that Zen's vital response to Nature, its expression of a love and veneration for all life, seems interestingly enough to be slowly developing a counterpart in the contemporary Western world. Although there appears to be no direct connection with ancient Zen tenets, the idea is gaining credence that plants, stones, trees, and flowers have "feelings" and can register their reaction to treatment by human beings. Many people now admit that they talk to their plants, comfort them when injured, encourage them to grow. Others have collections of "pet" rocks which receive special attention, reminding one of Zen lore, with its strict rules about the choosing, transporting and placing of stones in gardens where they are so often the focal point of the design. "A rock should be carefully considered before it is erected. Once it is put upright it should not be laid down and vice versa, to do so might upset the spirit of the rock."

The long misunderstood and neglected (by the Japanese themselves) flowerless stone-and-sand "meditation gardens" of Daisen-in and Ryoan-ji have become so famous in modern times that one finds them on every tourist's itinerary of celebrated Japanese sights. Japanese schoolchildren now so regularly troop through these cultural landmarks that, ironically enough, today the exact replica of the Ryoan-ji garden to be found in the Brooklyn Botanic

Garden in New York may well be the best place to view with some assurance and privacy this classic Zen design.

With Zen's enduring emphasis on Nature's lessons and the importance of the message which the natural world, if read properly, is able to convey, one would expect to find—and does find—many Zen stories that illustrate a concern which today might be designated as ecological. These old stories can be as minor as that of the dignified Zen master seen zealously pursuing, along a riverbank, a cabbage leaf which a careless cook had accidentally let fall into the water, or they can be more subtle, as in the story of the two monks traveling a long distance to the mountain retreat of a reputed sage. When the two monks neared their destination they were somewhat surprised to see a radish top floating down the stream along which their footpath was wandering. Their surprise was changed to mild dismay when they saw a second "wasted" radish top floating past. At the sight of the third radish top they turned back from their goal, realizing that they were not about to meet a "wise" personage, for the truly wise do not waste and are not careless.

Such simple stories, of which there are hundreds, reflect the Zen emphasis on "everyday life" as the real path to the great mystery. Master Joshu in replying to a disciple's question about the true nature of the Great Way, the Tao, replied, "Our everyday life, that is the Tao." In other words, the answer to one's meaning, one's direction and conduct is not hidden away in some arcane formula; it lies directly before you in the simplest terms.

> I draw water,
> I carry wood,
> This is my magic.

Zen's down-to-earthness has contributed to another of its singular attributes: its strong sense of humor, even humor at its own expense—a characteristic unquestionably unique in the history of religions. In Zen, laughter is not merely encouraged, it is in fact insisted upon as one way of keeping the human ego in its proper place in relation to the universe.

R. H. Blyth has written in his anthology *Oriental Humour*: "It is possible to read the Bible without a smile and the Koran without a chuckle; no one has died laughing while reading Buddhist sutras. But Zen writing abounds in anecdotes that stimulate the diaphragm. Enlightenment is frequently accompanied by laughter of a transcendental kind which may further be described as a laughter of surprised approval."

In humorous Zen anecdotes an event as unavoidable, as organic and above all as commonplace as death might be expected to—and does—find a place for itself. The Third Patriarch is said to have died standing upright with quietly clasped hands. Another great sage, after inquiring of his disciples "Who dies while sitting?" (*zazen*) and having received the unanimous answer "Enlightened monks," deliberately rose and, as if to ask the monks to question such behavioral stereotypes, began to walk up and down with his hands carelessly dangling at his sides in a very informal posture. On the seventh step he is reported to have expired with utmost composure. Another monk, named Ten Yin-feng, knowing he was about to die and determined to do so in some outstanding fashion, inquired if anyone had ever died standing up. Being assured that such an occurrence had indeed taken place, he then inquired, "How about upside down?" No one present had witnessed or even heard of such a demise, so Ten promptly stood on his head and thus gave up the ghost. His garments rose about his person, decorously covering his body, which remained in this headstand position so long that it became a public spectacle. Crowds of people traveled from near and far to view the phenomenon. These curiosity-seekers became a distinct inconvenience to Ten's fellow monks, who, how-

*Seated frog. Typical Zen irony at the expense of conventional pieties. The calligraphy reads:*

> *If you think by sitting*
> *[in a meditation posture]*
> *you can become a Buddha . . .*

*Kanzen and Jittoku (Chinese: Han-shan and Shi-te). Two famed Zen "idiots." Carefree followers of the simple life. Believers in the benefits of unrestrained laughter at the spectacle of the world's follies. Both paintings by Sengai (1750–1837).*

ever, could not agree among themselves about the disposal of the corpse. At last a Buddhist nun, who happened to be a younger sister of Ten's, arrived on the scene. Viewing her brother's corpse standing on its head, she addressed it with unconcealed annoyance: "While you were alive you took no proper notice of laws and cus-

toms and even now that you are dead you're making a thorough nuisance of yourself." Whereupon she gave the late Ten Yin-feng a sharp prod with her finger; his body fell over with a thud and she ordered it carted off to the burial grounds by his brothers.

Zen genuinely relishes laughter at its own expense, enjoying, in particular, anecdotes which expose sententiousness or pomposity. The typical reaction of a master to smug or self-assured behavior on the part of the pupil often seems to resemble a Mack Sennett or Marx Brothers comedy: a good swift kick in the behind, or some other devastating comic assault.

A monk came to the Master Ma Tsu for help in solving the *koan* he had been given: "What is the meaning of Bodhidharma's coming to China?" The Master suggested that before proceeding with the problem the monk should make him a low bow. As he was dutifully prostrating himself, Ma Tsu, the great Master, applied his foot to the monk's posterior. The unexpected kick resolved the murky irresolution in which the monk had been floundering for some time. When he felt the impact of his teacher's foot, he is said to have "attained immediate enlightenment." Subsequently he said to everyone he met, "Since I received that kick from Ma Tsu I haven't been able to stop laughing."

There is also the well-known exchange between the Master Sekkyo and one of his monks, in which the Master asked the monk:

"Can you take hold of empty space?"

"Yes, sir," the monk replied confidently.

"Show me how you do it."

The monk stretched out his arm and clutched at empty space.

Sekkyo remarked, "Is that the way? But after all you have not got anything."

"What then," inquired the monk, "is your way?"

*Young Zen monks sweeping the monastery garden paths as part of their Buddhist training.*

*Bodhidharma. A classic scene often represented in Japanese art: Bodhidharma facing the wall (of a cliff) during his long meditation. Behind him is the figure of Hui-k'o, the determined disciple who is said to have cut off his hand to prove the ardor of his intention to become Enlightened. Chinese. Thirteenth century. Artist unknown.*

The Master straightaway took hold of the monk's nose and gave it a hard pull.

The assailed monk cried out in pain, "Oh, oh, how hard you pull at my nose. You are hurting me terribly!"

"That is the way you have hold of empty space," said the Master.

Wry irony on the theme of empty ritualistic behavior also comes in for its share of zestful ridicule, as in the familiar story of the monk who on a wintry day in the monastery burned a wooden figure of a Buddha for warmth. Denounced for this sacrilege, he coolly replied that if the image had been the Buddha the special crystals called *sharira* would have appeared in the ashes. Since there were none he presumed that it was, after all, a piece of wood, and the day was extremely cold.

This scene of the Master cheerfully warming himself at the blaze was a favorite subject of Zen caricaturists. Another favorite was the two ragged, carefree Zen saints Kanzan and Jittoku, who are often described poking light-hearted fun at the formal piety of their brethren. These happy lunatics have apparently nothing better to do than stand around grinning delightedly at falling leaves, or the new moon, or birds quarreling over a worm. Jittoku and Kanzan are free, free as the ragged scarecrows of the fields which they resemble; and, as an old *haiku* reminds us:

> Even before His Majesty
> The scarecrow does not remove
> His plaited hat.

In summation, what can one finally say about Zen? It is not easy, it may in fact be impossible. One can only try. First, perhaps, it should be reaffirmed that there is in truth no goal to be attained. Even *satori*, enlightenment, is not to be imagined as something achieved after arduous effort. Arduous effort may be involved, to be sure, but it is not the real meaning. The real meaning, the real enlightenment, happens in the way a ripe fruit falls from a

*A monk depicted at a moment of* kensho *(sudden illumination; also known as* satori*). Polychrome-and-gold wooden sculpture, carved from a single block of wood. Chinese, Yuan dynasty, 1280–1368. Artist unknown.*

tree. All the effort of the seed struggling up through the soil, the
tree putting down roots and putting out branches, leaves, blossoms,
its patient endurance of the many opposing natural forces—all in
the end produce the fruit which, when fully ripe, silently, easily
falls. Yet, this whole process of fruition was a process, *not a goal*
and the seed itself was as much the goal, the *reality*, as the fruit
itself. The seed as seed is eternal; an apple seed is eternally an
apple seed, and given the chance it will become an apple tree producing more apple seed. As Dōgen said, wood is wood and ashes
are ashes. Wood has its own past, present and future, as also do
ashes. Enlightenment is, then, to live in accordance with one's
true nature. That is what the Buddha did. That is how he was
"Enlightened."

# Conclusion

*This Buddha and the three that follow (from Japan, Burma, India and Thailand) indicate the range of images one encounters in a survey of Buddhist art.*

*Buddha. Kamakura, Japan. Thirteenth century. Bronze.*

Since Buddhism is not a revealed religion and has always been a living and accumulative tradition, it has quite naturally gone through innumerable changes and developments in its long and varied history. Many minor sects and schools, different kinds of teaching, practice and philosophical emphasis, have been a part of the historic and cultural development of its two main branches, Hinayana and Mahayana—the latter including Tantrayana. Buddhism is not constructed on principles which make the charge of heresy quite as readily available as it was to Christianity in the past. In part, Buddhism's flexibility is, as already noted, rooted in the absence of any single, authoritarian, never-to-be questioned "Word of God." It derives from the firmly held Buddhist belief that man's mind is the creative center of his universe and that this mind has infinite capacity for change and growth. To hamper such possible development by the establishment of inalienable cosmological laws or epistemological and theological positions would not be relevant to the Buddhist point of view, for

*Buddha. India, Ellora Caves. Seventh century* A.D.
*Buddha. Burma. Early nineteenth century. Gilt bronze.*

Buddhism is not a single system of philosophy or a specific dogma set up counter to other dogmas. Instead, it is a path which the historic Buddha walked and which it is possible for any earnest human aspirant also to walk. This treading of a path that is open to all accounts for one of the Buddha's often-used titles, the *Tathagata*, meaning, as noted earlier, "one who has come and gone this way."

It is Buddhism's essential emphasis on man as the instrument of his own destiny which sets it apart from other world faiths. In his last words, spoken as he lay dying, the Buddha stated this in unequivocal terms, "Work out your own salvation with diligence. Be lamps unto yourselves."

These injunctions of the dying Buddha, with their strong psychological emphasis on man as the means of his own salvation, have sometimes led to the designation of Buddhism as a merely humanistic or even atheistic philosophy in which there is no place for any recognition of the "sacred." The Buddha did not construe Ultimate Reality in terms of a divine anthropomorphic image, and he did emphasize the futility of pursuing argumentatively the great abstract mysteries of the cosmos, preferring instead to hold man's gaze more directly on the fruitful living of daily life. Yet it is difficult to dismiss as either atheism or materialism the teachings of a Master who could state, as quoted earlier, "There is an unborn, an unoriginated, an unmade, an uncompounded. Were there not, O mendicants, there would be no escape from the world of the born, the originated, the made and the compounded."

In the forms of Buddhism discussed in this book, the Buddha is not conceived of as a Messiah or a Savior but only as an awakened and perfected or completed person, the discoverer of a universal truth to which he devoted more than forty years in passing on to others—always, however, with the firm injunction that they themselves "must walk the Way." This Middle Way, a progressive course of development, mental, moral, physical and spiritual, is the basic teaching of the Theravada School. It is also the fundamental structure on which the Mahayana (including Tantrayana) has built its own expanded forms of discipline and instruction.

The *Sangha,* that brotherhood of followers which visibly and formally leads the Buddha's way of "life for others," is said to be the oldest monastic order in the world. Established to teach and test the Buddha's discoveries, it has often been compared to a hospital where the patients come to be cured of the "disease" of a limited and demanding ego. In this metaphor, the tenets of the Buddha's Laws for Living are seen as the prescription for a cure which depends on the faithful following of an Eightfold Path or Middle Way, with specified activities and awarenesses through which the individual learns to free himself of the hampering bonds of that universal human sickness, egocentrism.

Despite Buddhism's essential emphasis on man's own consciousness as the creative center of the universe, or, one might fairly say, *because of* this emphasis, one can find in Buddhism a number of props and supports for the ordinary individual who is earnestly attempting to walk the Middle Way. We have suggested in the preceding pages some of the kinds of "skillful means" by which Buddhism as taught in the Theravada, Tantrayana and Zen schools has adapted itself to the incontrovertible fact that human beings are not all at the same stage of development.

Although Buddhism abounds in contradictions and paradoxes, Buddhists in general do not seem to be bothered by them. The proliferation of Buddhist deities which is such an integral aspect of Buddhist art in certain cultures clearly illustrates this point. The creation of a religious pantheon abounding in gods, demons, celestial nymphs, angels, nature spirits and numerous *Bodhisattvas* may seem to purists a long way from the uncompromising simplicity of the original teachings. Buddhism, however, without embarrassment, accepts this phenomenon as an activity common to the human imagination everywhere. In the West, where we ostensibly deplore "gods" and have been taught the error of creating graven images, we are apt to be myopic about our own propensity to deify Science, Technology, Medicine. We tend to regard them as superpersonal agencies producing sacrosanct dogma capable of solving, or at least ameliorating, our immediate human problems.

If we were to set out on a trip to the pilgrimage sites of Buddhism, we would inevitably encounter "relics." The great golden

Shwedagon Pagoda in Rangoon, Burma, houses, so it is alleged, a few of Buddha's hairs, and one of his teeth is enshrined on the island of Sri Lanka in the Temple of the Tooth at Kandy. For some reason, the tooth relic is hard for Western critics to accept with equanimity, particularly if their reading has informed them that the Portuguese destroyed this sacred object when they were attempting to stamp out "heathenism" in the Asian world. The disputed tooth is, however, no more and no less believable than the "true" fragments of the Christian Cross or threads from a garment of the Virgin Mary which many devout Catholics have no difficulty in venerating as symbols of a "holy reality" of the distant past.

I personally am never confronted with a bewildered or even outraged reaction to the enshrinement of one of the Buddha's teeth without recalling an old Chinese Buddhist story about a devout elderly lady who, on learning that a neighbor was soon to make the momentous trip to distant India to the very birthplace of the Buddha himself, beseeched the traveler to bring back to her some relic of the Great Teacher. It did not matter how trivial—she would erect a shrine to it and she and her friends would go daily to worship there. Because of her advanced age and her extreme piety the traveler hadn't the heart to refuse her request. He did not, however, give the matter another thought until he was nearing home on the last lap of his great journey. Then walking along in chagrin, asking himself what he could do to redeem his solemn promise, he spied beside the road the corpse of a dog. He went to the corpse, removed one of the dog's teeth and, wrapping it carefully in a small piece of fine silk, brought it to the old woman. Overjoyed at the gift, she erected the shrine as promised, and went there daily with her friends to worship. In time a subtle effulgence was seen to emanate from the enshrined dog's tooth. The single-hearted devotion, humility and gratitude of the old lady had indeed produced a miracle.

Miracles are possible in Buddhism, even though the Buddha discouraged all display of miraculous or parapsychological powers as offering proof of spiritual attainment. He was first and foremost a pragmatist, a patient compassionate pragmatist. A story that is told of his response to a noted fakir whose path he crossed on one of his journeys nicely illustrates his down-to-earth reaction to any extremes of yogic behavior. Encountering an ascetic practitioner of hatha yoga at a river crossing, he entered into conversation as he often did when traveling, and was told that the yogin had achieved such mastery over his physical body that he could now cross the river walking on the water. The Buddha's comment was to the effect that such a feat, though remarkable of its kind, seemed a rather useless expenditure of physical and psychological energy, since there was a good ferry crossing the river at regular intervals charging less than a penny for the ride.*

The Buddha was, as we have seen, consistently opposed to authoritarianism. He sought to free man from the bonds of the accepted, the customary. He stressed effort; right effort. Laziness and torpor were as much to be avoided as evil desires. Desire, indeed, in Buddhist terms, need not be a bad thing. It is possible to desire good; even "struggle" to attain it. The word "struggle" is pertinent. In some of the old scriptures the word "wrestling" is used to describe the effort to gain release from false craving and false views.

In general, the Buddha's teaching involved what could be termed "a change of method." He taught a way of living life. In teaching this, he refused to be sidetracked by argumentation on two kinds of subjects: those not deemed solvable by the human intellect—no matter how acute—and those that were, in his view, not vitally central but merely accessory.

From the outset there was never a persecuting spirit in Buddhism; no churchly support (as in Islam, and also, sadly enough, in some branches of Judaism and Christianity) endorsed the notion that differences in belief constituted an offense against an Almighty Divine Power—a concept which has tacitly encouraged the theory that "infidels" should be converted by brute force if necessary, or at least permitted to continue their mistaken way only through the sufferance of a superior "righteous" power, sole custodian of ultimate truth.

---

* This anecdote has also been attributed to Sri Ramakrishna. My authority is Dr. Edward Conze in his book *Buddhism: Its Essence and Development*, where it is attributed to the Buddha.

More than 2,500 years ago the Buddha attempted to turn human beings toward a clearer knowledge of their own constitution and psychological capacities. In the Buddha's view, human destiny was not determined by some omniscient Divinity existing well outside the confines of an "evil" world. Instead it lay within each individual's power to affect; a power achieved by understanding and, above all, by *practice* translated in terms of personal willingness, will and effort.

*Buddha. Thailand. Seventh century* A.D. *Bronze.*

# Appendixes

*Appendix I*

From *The Tantric Mysticism of Tibet* by John Blofeld
E. P. Dutton & Co., Inc., New York, 1970, pp. 194–95.

. . . mantra recitation constitutes the main practice of farmers and artisans who need a form of devotion-cum-meditation for use at work. It is at once a simple and very effective technique. Of mantras used in this way, the Mani is by far the commonest and will serve as an example of them all. It consists of the six syllables *Om Mani Padme Hum*, to which so much meaning is attached that the Lama Govinda's attempt to explain them developed into a book of three hundred pages!

In common with all mantras, the Mani has *Om* as its first syllable. *Om* stands for the totality of sound and, indeed, for the totality of existence. Originally written *Aum*, it starts at the back of the throat and ends with the lips. It is chief among the sounds to which a mystical creative quality is attached. Translators who have rendered it 'O,' 'Oh' or 'Hail' have obviously misconceived its meaning and its function. The A stands for consciousness of the external world; the U, for consciousness of what goes on inside our minds; and the M, for consciousness of the non-dual, unqualified emptiness of the void.

The next syllable is *Mani*, meaning the Jewel. It is equated with Vajra, the adamantine non-substance which is perfectly void and yet more impervious to harm or change than the hardest substance known to chemistry. *Mani* is the symbol of highest value within our own mind, the pure void which is always to be found there when the intervening layers of murky consciousness are pierced.

*Padma* (of which *Padme* is the vocative form) literally means the Lotus. It is the symbol of spiritual unfoldment whereby the *Mani* is finally reached.

*Hum*, like *Om*, is untranslatable. *Om* is the infinite and *Hum* is the infinite within the finite and therefore stands for our potential Enlightenment, the perception of the void within the non-void, Mind in the form of mind, the unconditioned in the conditioned, the transcendental in the ephemeral, the subtle embodied in the dense. This above all other mantric syllables symbolizes the central truth of the Vajrayana—the truth of voidness enclosed within the petals of non-void.

*Om* and *Hum*, however, are much more than symbols. Properly used, they have the power to awake in the human consciousness an intuitive understanding of truths impossible to clothe in words. *Mani Padme*, the Jewel and the Lotus which form the body of the mantra, have, even at the surface level, a number of complementary meanings. For example, the Lotus stands for the Dharma and the Jewel for the liberating truth it enfolds; or the Lotus is the world of form and the Jewel, the formless world, the reality infusing form; and so on.

*Appendix II*

Sakyamuni Coming Out from the Mountain

*Liang Kai, Southern Sung*

He drags his bare feet
    out of a cave
        under a tree,
eyebrows
    grown long with weeping
        and hooknosed woe,
in ragged soft robes
    wearing a fine beard,
        unhappy hands
clasped to his naked breast—
    humility is beatness
        humility is beatness—
faltering
    into the bushes by a stream,
        all things inanimate
but his intelligence—
    stands upright there
        tho trembling:
Arhat
    who sought Heaven
        under a mountain of stone,
sat thinking
    till he realized
        the land of blessedness exists
in the imagination—
    the flash come:
        empty mirror—
how painful to be born again
    wearing a fine beard,
        reentering the world
a bitter wreck of a sage:
    earth before him his only path.
        We can see his soul,
he knows nothing
    like a god:
        shaken
meek wretch—
    humility is beatness
        before the absolute World.

ALLEN GINSBERG
New York Public Library 1953

# Glossary

Where there was a choice between the Pali and Sanskrit forms of a term, the author has in general chosen the one more commonly used—thus, *tanha* (Pali) rather than *trishna* (Sanskrit), but *dharma* (Sanskrit) instead of *dhamma* (Pali).

Diacritical marks have been omitted throughout this text because they are unfamiliar to the average reader. In a number of words, therefore, the spelling has included an "h," as in *Avalokiteshvara, shakti, Shiva,* to indicate the proper pronunciation. The use of upper or lower case in such words as Enlightenment, Awakening and *Bodhisattva* has depended upon the context in which they appear.

*Abhidhamma:* Pali for the Higher Dhamma or Teaching, a part of the canon of the Theravada School. It consists of philosophical and psychological material. Sanskrit: *Abhidharma.*

*Amida:* A Japanese name for the Buddha of the Pure Realm. See also *Amitabha.*

*Amitabha:* Another name for the Buddha of the Pure Realm or the Buddha of Boundless Light and Compassion.

*anatta:* Buddhist term for nonego. Absence of a permanent unchanging self or soul.

*anicca:* The Buddhist teaching of the law of impermanence, a characteristic of all existence in Buddhist thought.

*arahat, arhat* or *arahant:* The ideal of Hinayana (Theravada) Buddhism; one who has freed himself from all ego cravings and thus attained enlightenment.

*asanas:* Bodily postures used in Hindu and Buddhist meditation.

*Aum* (also spelled *Om*): Sacred syllable or *mantra* used in higher forms of invocation or meditation.

*Avalokiteshvara:* Personification of the self-generative creative cosmic force (Humphreys); also called Padmapani, Kuan Yin or Kwannon.

*avidya:* Ignorance.

*Bardo:* The after-death state which forms the theme of the Tibetan *Bardo Thödol,* or Book of the Dead.

*bhakti:* Devotion, worship of a god through personal love.

*bhikkhu:* A member of the Buddhist *Sangha* in Theravada lands.

*bodhi:* A term used in both Sanskrit and Pali meaning perfect wisdom or enlightenment.

*Bodhidharma:* An Indian missionary monk who came to China in the sixth century A.D. Regarded as the founder of the Ch'an (Zen) School of Buddhism. (Known in Japan as Daruma.)

*Bodhisattva:* In Mahayana Buddhism, one who having attained enlightenment (*bodhi*) is on his way to Buddhahood but postpones his goal to keep a vow to help all life attain salvation.

*Bodhi Tree:* The tree under which the Buddha attained Enlightenment. Sometimes referred to as the Bo Tree.

*Bön:* Animistic, shamanistic religion of Tibet, preceding Buddhism and influencing it.

*Brahma:* God as creator; a *mythological* concept; member of the classic Hindu triad of gods: Brahma-Vishnu-Shiva.

*Brahman:* The Supreme Principle of Life; a *metaphysical* term. (Name also sometimes given to members of the priestly Hindu caste.)

*Brahmin:* Name used in the present text for the priestly caste of Hindus.

*Buddha:* An Awakened One. Refers usually to Siddhartha Gautama, the Indian prince who became an All-Enlightened Being, the historic founder of Buddhism.

*buddhi:* Wisdom in the sense of highly developed intuition, the principle through which pure consciousness is reflected.

*chakra:* A wheel; in yoga, one of the psychic centers of the body.

*Ch'an:* Chinese name for Zen. (See also *dhyana.*)

*cha-no-yu:* Term for the Japanese tea ceremony. Literally, tea and water.

*Dalai Lama:* The periodically incarnated spiritual and temporal head of the country of Tibet, now in exile since the Chinese Communist invasion.

*Daruma:* Japanese name for the First Zen Patriarch, Bodhidharma.

*Dependent Origination:* Theory of the chain of causation by which *karma* is carried on; teaching central to Hinayana Buddhism.

*dhamma:* Pali word for righteousness, duty, law. See *dharma.*

*Dhammapada:* A collection of Buddhist teachings; a part of the Pali canon of Hinayana (Theravada) Buddhism.

*dharma:* Sanskrit word (*dhamma* in Pali) used in both Hinduism and Buddhism, meaning variously, according to context, the way, the law, righteousness, reality. "The path which a man should follow in accordance with his nature and station in life."

*dhyana:* Sanskrit word for dynamic meditation or contemplation leading to enlightenment. (The words *Ch'an* and *Zen* are transliterations of *dhyana.*)

*dorje:* Tibetan word for thunderbolt; a symbol used in Tibetan religious art and ritual. See *vajra.*

*dukkha:* Buddhist word meaning suffering, pain, "dislocation."

*Eightfold Path:* Buddhism's formulation of the eight steps necessary for "awakening."

*emptiness:* See *sunyata.*

*Enlightenment:* In Buddhist usage, refers to the experiencing of one's own essential or true nature and therefore awakening to the nature of all existence, as in the Buddha's "awakening" under the Bo Tree.

*Eternal Now:* Buddhist teaching about "living in the moment."

*Existentialism:* Modern Western philosophy emphasizing man's responsibility for his personal life through the choices he makes.

*First Patriarch of Zen:* See *Bodhidharma.*

*Four Noble Truths:* The Buddha's teaching that (1) existence involves inevitable suffering for all people; (2) this suffering springs from egocentrism; (3) egocentrism can be rooted out; (4) this rooting out can come by following the Eightfold Path.

*Four Signs:* In Buddhist legend, also the Four Sights—an old man, a diseased man, a corpse and a holy man—which influenced Prince Siddhartha Gautama to leave his luxurious home and go forth on the search for enlightenment that led him to Buddhahood.

*Gandhara:* Sanskrit name for an Indian district, now part of Pakistan and Afghanistan, famous for early Buddha images in Greco-Roman style.

*Gautama:* Family name of the historic Buddha; also spelled Gotama.

*geshe:* An exceptionally knowledgeable Tibetan guru; a ranking equivalent to a Doctor of Divinity.

*Gotama:* See *Gautama.*

*Great Demise:* Term for the Buddha's death.

*Great Departure:* Buddhist term for Siddhartha's departure from his father's palace.

*Great Renunciation:* The silent and secret leave-taking from his family, including his wife and infant son, of Siddhartha Gautama, the Buddha-to-be.

*haiku:* Seventeen-syllable Japanese poem.

*hara:* Specifically the lower abdomen, considered the body-mind's vital center from which all the body's energies should properly radiate. (See *tanden.*)

*hatha yoga:* The yoga path that leads to release through union of the mind with the body.

*Hinayana Buddhism:* The "Lesser Vehicle of Buddhism" as compared to the "Larger Vehicle," Mahayana; refers to the scope and range of interpretation and permissiveness in relation to the Buddha's doctrine. See *Theravada Buddhism,* preferable term.

*Isness:* Term used in Zen to emphasize the immediate state of being.

*Jatakas:* A collection of Indian folk stories about the Buddha's former lives.

*"Joshu's Mu":* Famed Zen master Joshu's classic reply to a question that was put to him by a fellow monk; one of the famous *koans* of Zen. (The Chinese term is *wu.*)

*judo:* A Japanese method of weaponless offense and defense built on principles of nonaggression.

*jujitsu:* Another name for judo; *ju* means gentle, *jitsu,* art or practice.

*kalpa:* An eon, a vast period of time that encompasses the creation and dissolution of a universe.

*kamma* (Pali): See *karma* (Sanskrit).

*karma:* Literally, "action"; the law of cause and effect, sometimes interpreted personally as punishment or reward for deeds performed in former lives.

*karma yoga:* The yoga path that leads to release through selfless activity.

*karuna:* The Mahayana Buddhist term for compassion; a trait of *Bodhisattvas.*

*Kegon:* A school of Buddhism.

*kendo:* Japanese swordsmanship.

*kensho:* Seeing into one's own nature, or the first experience of *satori,* "awakening."

*kinhin:* Formal walking meditation designed in part to loosen joints stiff from sitting meditation.

*koan:* A Japanese term used in Rinzai Zen taken from the Chinese *kung-an,* meaning a public document. In Zen, it suggests a word or a phrase couched in irrational language which cannot be solved by intellectual processes but whose meaning must burst on the mind directly. *Koans* are used as exercises in breaking the patterns of so-called thought, developing instead deep intuition and achieving a state of awareness beyond that of duality; in other words, attaining *kensho* or *satori.*

*Kshatriya:* The Buddha's caste. The second of India's four major castes; rulers and aristocrats.

*Kuan-yin* (or *Kwan-yin*): Chinese name for the *Bodhisattva* known in Indian Buddhism as Avalokiteshvara; often presented in female form.

*Kwannon:* Japanese name for the *Bodhisattva* Kuan-yin.

*lama:* Tibetan term for a Buddhist monk or spiritual leader.

*Mahayana:* A Buddhist term meaning "Larger Vehicle," applied in general to the northern Buddhism of Tibet, Mongolia, China, Korea, Japan. It has many schools and forms.

*Maitreya:* The Buddha of the Future.

*mandala:* A diagrammatic circular picture used as an aid in meditation or ritual; sometimes a symbol of the universe, or a representation of a deed of merit.

*mani walls:* Name given to the walls in Himalayan Buddhist countries which have been painted with the words *Om mani padme hum* (Hail to the Jewel in the Lotus). See Appendix I.

*Manjusri:* The *Bodhisattva* of Meditation, whose image—as personification of Supreme Wisdom—is usually seen in Zen meditation halls.

*mantra* (or *mantram*): A Sanskrit term used in both Buddhism and Hinduism signifying a sacred word, verse or syllable which embodies in sound some specific deity or supernatural power.

*maya:* A word used in both Buddhism and Hinduism signifying the "illusion" of the world's appearance.

*merit:* A Buddhist term used in connection with the performance of good deeds.

*metta:* Pali word meaning loving-kindness; the basis of a meditation in the Theravada School of Buddhism and the subject of the *Metta Sutta.*

*Middle Way:* Buddhism's description of the path lying between all extremes as, for instance, asceticism and self-indulgence; advocated by the Buddha as the proper path for man to follow.

*mindfulness:* Buddhist term; "awareness."

*mondo:* Japanese word used in Zen; a rapid-fire question-and-answer technique employed to overcome conventional conceptual thought patterns.

*mudra:* A mystic or symbolic gesture of hand and fingers.

*Naga:* A snake deity.

*nazuna:* The name of a Japanese flowering weed, used in a famous *haiku.*

*Nibbana:* Pali word meaning Nirvana.

*Nirvana:* The attainment of final enlightenment; freedom from rebirth.

*No drama:* The ancient drama of Japan, rooted in Zen concepts.

*Om:* The most sacred *mantra* of the Vedas. (See *Aum.*)

# GLOSSARY

*Om mani padme hum:* Hail to the Jewel in the Lotus. A Tibetan mantra recited by devotees, also painted on the so-called mani walls. See Appendix I.

*Padmapani:* A name for the *Bodhisattva* Avalokiteshvara: "lotus carrier," or lotus-born.

*Padmasana:* Classic yoga pose.

*Pali:* The language of the Theravada (Hinayana) Buddhist canon, alleged to be the language used by the Buddha, or similar to it.

*Parinirvana:* The final or perfect Nirvana, ending all earthly existences, implying no further rebirth.

*Pitaka:* Literally, "basket"; the three *Pitakas*, or the *Tripitaka*, represent the main body of the Pali canon of Buddhism.

*prajna:* Wisdom; spiritual awakening.

*reincarnation:* Belief in the living of more than one life.

*rinpoche:* Tibetan Buddhist teacher and guide, the equivalent of *roshi* in Zen Buddhism.

*Rinzai:* One of the two main schools of Zen Buddhism, in which training involves the use of the *koan* and *mondo.*

*roshi:* The name given to a Zen master of a monastery, one who gives Zen instruction to pupil-monks.

*sabi:* Japanese word meaning rustic unpretentiousness, as in the standards of taste applied to the tea ceremony.

*Sakyamuni:* See *Shakyamuni.*

*samsara:* The ceaseless round of becoming; the life of phenomena; opposite of Nirvana.

*Sangha:* The Buddhist monastic order, also, more generally, any community practicing the Buddhist way.

*sanzen:* An important part of Rinzai Zen training, a brief charged interview between master and student, usually involving the student's *koan.*

*Satipatthana:* The name of an intensive type of meditation practiced in Theravada Buddhism.

*satori:* Deep enlightenment, awakening to the truth beyond dualism and discrimination.

*sesshin:* Period of intensive prolonged meditation practiced in Zen, in total silence; designed to concentrate and unify the mind; usual *sesshin* period lasts three to seven days.

*shabda:* "Spiritual" sound of a *mantra.*

*shakti:* Energy, force.

*Shakya:* The name of the Buddha's "clan."

*Shakyamuni:* "The sage of the Shakya clan"—one of the Buddha's various titles.

*sharira:* A special crystal substance allegedly found in the cremated remains of saints; relic.

*Shinto:* The indigenous religion of Japan.

*sitting:* A term used in Soto Zen in reference to meditative practice.

*skandha:* The five aggregates which, in Buddhist terms, make up an individual.

*Soto:* Zen sect which stresses quiet meditation and "sitting with awareness"; founded by Dōgen, who brought Chinese Zen teachings to his homeland, Japan, in 1127.

*stupa:* Originally a mound for relics, in particular the Buddha's; developed into elaborate architectural forms: *chortens, dagobas, pagodas.*

*sunyata:* The void, or emptiness; "the dynamic substratum of all existence" (Kapleau); a basic teaching in certain schools of Buddhism, Zen in particular.

*sutra:* The Sanskrit word for Buddhist scriptures, meaning a discourse by the Buddha, or a disciple, accepted as authoritative teaching; often a short sentence containing highly condensed teaching; literal meaning—"a thread on which jewels are hung."

*sutta:* The pali word for *sutra,* or scriptures.

*tanden:* A Zen term for a center of "awareness" in the abdominal region; used in certain meditative practices and in judo instruction. (See *hara.*)

*tanha:* Pali for craving or thirst; in Buddhism, the cause of rebirth; see also *trishna.*

*Tantra* or *Tantras:* A body of esoteric Hindu religious literature said to have been revealed by the god Shiva for man's guidance in the present age, i.e., the Kali Yuga. These scriptures place emphasis on the worship of the female essence of the universe, the Divine Mother, or *shakti.* (See also *Mahayana.*)

*Tantrayana:* A school of esoteric Tibetan Buddhism; also called *Vajrayana,* it emphasizes not only meditation but also the use of symbolic rites, gestures, postures, breathing, incantation and other secret formulas.

*Tathagata:* A name for the Buddha meaning "one who has come and gone *thus,*" or "one who has followed the ancient Path."

*tea ceremony:* The formal Japanese way of serving tea; related to Zen meditative practices.

*Theravada Buddhism:* The School of the Elders, another—and preferred— term for the Hinayana or Southern school of Buddhism: Sri Lanka, Thailand, Burma. *Thera* means "elders."

*Tipitaka* (Pali for *Tripitaka*): Literally, the "Three Baskets"; the basis of the Pali canon of Theravada Buddhism.

*Tripitaka:* See preceding.

*trishna:* Sanskrit for craving, grasping, clinging; see also *tanha.*

*ushnisha:* The cranial protuberance on top of the Buddha's head; one of the marks of his supernatural anatomy.

*vajra:* Sanskrit for the thunderbolt symbol used in Tibetan religious art and ritual, representing the "force of adamantine truth."

*Vajrayana:* Way of the Vajra, or "adamantine truth," in Tibetan Buddhist tradition.

*vihara:* Theravada Buddhist term for a dwelling place for monks.

*wabi:* A Japanese term meaning simplicity, unpretentiousness, implying not being "in the swim," not trying to "keep up with the Joneses"; a tea-ceremony term.

*yantra:* A magic diagram.

*zazen:* Sitting meditation; a type of Zen discipline.

*Zen:* One of the main schools of Japanese Buddhism, original Japanese pronunciation of the Chinese ideograph Ch'an, derived from Sanskrit *dhyana.*

*zendo:* A room in which Zen meditation is practiced.

# Bibliography

Anderson, Walt, *Open Secrets, A Western Guide to Tibetan Buddhism*. New York: The Viking Press, 1979.

Anesaki, Masaharu, *A History of Buddhist Art*. Boston: Houghton Mifflin Co., 1915.

————, *History of Japanese Religion*. Rutland, Vt.: Charles E. Tuttle, 1963.

Argüelles, José and Miriam, *Mandala*. Berkeley and London: Shambhala, 1972.

Beal, Samuel, *Buddhist Records of the Western World* (tr. from the Chinese of Hiuen Tsiang, A.D. 629). London: Kegan Paul, Trench, Trubner & Co., undated.

Blofeld, John, *The Tantric Mysticism of Tibet*. New York: E. P. Dutton & Co., Inc., 1970.

————, *The Wheel of Life*. Boulder, Colo.: Shambhala, 1978.

————, *The Zen Teaching of Huang Po (on the Transmission of Mind)*. New York: Grove Press, Inc., 1959.

Blyth, R. H., *Haiku*. 4 vols. Tokyo: Hokuseido Press, 1950.

————, *Oriental Humour*. Tokyo: Hokuseido Press, 1959.

————, *Zen in English Literature and Oriental Classics*. Tokyo: Hokuseido Press, 1942.

Bowie, Henry P., *On the Laws of Japanese Painting*. New York: Dover, 1911. Reprinted by Peter Smith.

Bowie, Theodore, ed., *The Arts of Thailand*. Bloomington, Ind.: Indiana University Press, 1960.

Burtt, E. A., ed., *The Teachings of the Compassionate Buddha*. New York: Mentor Religious Classics, New American Library, 1955.

Capra, Fritjof, *The Tao of Physics*. Berkeley, Calif.: Shambhala, 1975.

Chang, Chen-Chi, *The Practice of Zen*. New York: Harper & Brothers, 1959.

Chang, Garma C. C., *The Buddhist Teaching of Totality*. University Park, Pa., and London: The Pennsylvania State University Press, 1971.

Conze, Edward, *Buddhism: Its Essence and Development*. New York: Harper Torchbooks, 1959.

Conze, E., Horner, I. B., Snellgrove, D., and Waley, A., eds., *Buddhist Texts Through the Ages*. Oxford: Bruno Cassirer, Ltd., 1954.

Coomaraswamy, Ananda, *Buddha and the Gospel of Buddhism*. London: George G. Harrap & Co., 1941. Reprinted by South Asia Books, 1974.

Coomaraswamy, Ananda, and The Sister Nivedita (Margaret E. Noble), *Myths and Legends of the Hindus and Buddhists.* London: George G. Harrap & Co., 1913. Reprinted by Peter Smith.

David-Neel, Alexandra, *Initiations and Initiates in Tibet.* London: Rider & Co., 1931.

————, *With Mystics and Magicians in Tibet.* New York: Penguin Books, 1931, and University Books, Inc., 1964.

de Bary, Wm. Theodore, *Buddhist Tradition in India, China and Japan.* New York: Random House, 1972.

————, *Sources of the Japanese Tradition.* New York: Columbia University Press, 1958.

Desjardins, Arnaud, *The Message of the Tibetans.* London: Stuart & Watkins, 1969.

Dumoulin, Heinrich, S.J., *A History of Zen Buddhism.* New York: Pantheon Books, 1963, and Beacon Press, 1969.

Eliot, Sir Charles, *Hinduism and Buddhism.* 3 vols. London: Routledge & Kegan Paul Ltd., 1954.

Evans-Wentz, W. Y., tr., *The Tibetan Book of the Dead.* London: Oxford University Press, 1951.

Gordon, Antoinette K., *The Iconography of Tibetan Lamaism.* Rev. edition. Rutland, Vt., and Tokyo, Japan: Charles E. Tuttle Co., Inc., 1959.

————, *Tibetan Religious Art.* New York: Columbia University Press, 1952.

Govinda, Lama Anagarika, *Foundations of Tibetan Mysticism.* New York: Samuel Weiser, 1969.

————, *The Way of the White Clouds.* Berkeley, Calif.: Shambhala, 1970.

Graham, Dom Aelred, *Conversations: Christian and Buddhist.* New York: Harcourt, Brace & World, Inc., 1968.

————, *Zen Catholicism.* New York: Harcourt, Brace & World, Inc., 1963.

Griswold, A. B., *King Mongkut of Siam.* New York: The Asia Society, 1961.

Guenther, Herbert V., and Trungpa, Chögyam, *The Dawn of Tantra.* The Clear Light Series. Berkeley and London: Shambhala, 1975.

Hall, H. Fielding, *The Soul of a People.* London: Macmillan & Co., Ltd., 1899. (About Burma.)

Hamilton-Merritt, Jane, *A Meditator's Diary.* New York: Harper & Row, Inc., 1976.

Harada, Jiro, *Japanese Gardens.* Boston: Charles T. Branford Company, 1956.

Herrigel, Eugen, *Zen in the Art of Archery.* New York: Pantheon Books, Inc., 1953.

Hisamatsu, Shin'Ichi, *Zen and the Fine Arts.* Tokyo: Kodansha International, Ltd., 1974.

Hoover, Thomas, *Zen Culture.* New York: Random House, 1977.

Humphreys, Christmas, *Buddhism.* England: Penguin Books, 1951.

————, *Zen Buddhism.* London: William Heinemann, Ltd., 1949.

Ikemoto, Takashi, and Stryk, Lucien, *Zen Poems, Prayers, Sermons, Anecdotes, Interviews.* New York: Anchor Books, Doubleday & Co., Inc., 1965.

Jung, Carl G., and Wilhelm, Richard, *The Secret of the Golden Flower.* New York: Harcourt, Brace & Company, 1938.

Kapleau, Philip, *The Three Pillars of Zen.* New York and Evanston, Ill.: Harper & Row, 1966.

————, *Zen: Dawn in the West*. Garden City, N.Y.: Anchor Press/Doubleday, 1979.

Kuck, Loraine E., *The Art of Japanese Gardens*. New York: The John Day Company, 1940.

Lee, Sherman E., *A History of Far Eastern Art*. New York: Harry N. Abrams, Inc., 1963.

————, *Tea Taste in Japanese Art*. New York: The Asia Society, Inc., 1963. Reprinted by Arno Press, 1979.

Ling, Trevor, *The Buddha*. New York: Charles Scribner's Sons, 1973.

Maraini, Fosco, *Secret Tibet*. New York: Viking Press, 1952.

Mitchell, Elsie, *Sun Buddha, Moon Buddha*. New York and Tokyo: Weatherhill, 1973.

Morgan, Kenneth W., ed., *The Path of Buddha: Buddhism Interpreted by Buddhists*. New York: The Ronald Press Company, 1956.

Morris, Ivan, *The World of the Shining Prince: Court Life in Ancient Japan*. New York: Alfred A. Knopf, 1964, and Penguin Books, 1971.

Murasaki, Lady, *The Tale of Genji*. Boston and New York: Houghton Mifflin Company, 1935; New York: Anchor Books.

Needleman, Jacob, *The New Religions*. Garden City, N.Y.: Doubleday, 1970; New York: E. P. Dutton, 1977.

Norbu, Thubten Jigme [the brother of the Dalai Lama], *Tibet Is My Country*. New York: E. P. Dutton & Co., 1961.

Pagels, Elaine, *The Gnostic Gospels*. New York: Random House, 1979.

Pallis, Marco, *Peaks and Lamas*. Rev. ed. New York: Alfred A. Knopf, Inc., 1949.

Pratt, J. B., *The Pilgrimage of Buddhism*. New York: The Macmillan Co., 1928.

Prebish, Charles S., ed., *Buddhism, A Modern Perspective*. University Park, Pa., and London: The Pennsylvania State University Press, 1975.

Reischauer, A. K., *Studies in Japanese Buddhism*. New York: The Macmillan Company, 1917. Reprinted by AMS Press, 1970.

Ross, Nancy Wilson, ed. and contributor, *The World of Zen*. New York: Random House, 1960; Vintage, 1964.

————, *Three Ways of Asian Wisdom*. New York: Simon and Schuster, 1966.

Rowland, Benjamin, Jr., *The Evolution of the Buddha Image*. New York: The Asia Society, Inc., 1962. Reprinted by Arno Press, 1979.

Saddhatissa, H., *The Buddha's Way*. New York: George Braziller, 1971.

Sadler, A. L., *Cha-no-yu: The Japanese Tea Ceremony*. Rutland, Vt.: Charles E. Tuttle, 1977.

Sansom, Sir George, *Japan: A Short Cultural History*. New York: Appleton-Century-Crofts, 1962. Reprinted by Stanford University Press.

Sasaki, Ruth Fuller, *Zen: A Religion*. New York: The First Zen Institute of America, 1958.

Schloegel, Irmgard, *The Wisdom of the Zen Masters*. New York: New Directions Publishing Corp., 1975.

Schumacher, E. F., *Small Is Beautiful*. New York: Harper & Row, Perennial Library, 1975.

Seckel, Dietrich, *The Art of Buddhism*. Art of the World Series. New York: Crown Publishers, Inc., 1964.

Shattock, E. H., *An Experiment in Mindfulness*. New York: Samuel Weiser, n.d.

Shway Yoe (Sir James Scott), *The Burman: His Life and Notions*. New York: W. W. Norton & Company, 1963.

Smith, Huston, *The Religions of Man*. New York: Harper & Row, Inc., 1958.

Suzuki, Daisetz Teitaro, *The Essence of Buddhism*. London: The Buddhist Society, 1947.

————, *The Essentials of Zen Buddhism* (selected writings of Daisetz T. Suzuki, ed. and with an introduction by Bernard Phillips). New York: E. P. Dutton & Co., 1962, and Greenwood, 1973.

————, *Zen and Japanese Culture*. New York: Bollingen Foundation, Inc., Pantheon Books, Inc., 1959.

————, *Zen Buddhism* (selected writings of D. T. Suzuki, ed. and with an introduction by William Barrett). New York: Anchor Books, Doubleday & Company, Inc., 1956.

Suzuki, Shunryu, *Zen Mind, Beginner's Mind* (informal talks on Zen meditation and practice by Shunryu Suzuki Roshi, ed. by Trudy Dixon with an introduction by Richard Baker). New York and Tokyo: Weatherhill, 1970.

Swearer, Donald K., ed., *Secrets of the Lotus*. New York: The Macmillan Co., 1971.

Thomas, E. J., *The Life of Buddha as Legend and History*. New York: Barnes & Noble, Inc., 1960; London: Routledge & Kegan Paul, 1969.

Thomas, E. J., and Francis, H. T., eds., *Jataka Tales*. England: Cambridge University Press, 1916.

Thomas, Lewis, *The Lives of a Cell*. New York: Bantam Books, Inc., 1975.

Tompkins, Peter, and Bird, Christopher, *The Secret Life of Plants*. New York: Harper and Row, 1973.

Trungpa, Chögyam, *Born in Tibet*. New York: A Helen & Kurt Wolff Book. Harcourt Brace & World, Inc., 1968; Berkeley, Calif.: Shambhala, 1978.

————, *Cutting Through Spiritual Materialism*. The Clear Light Series. Berkeley: Shambhala, 1973.

————, *Meditation in Action*. The Clear Light Series. Berkeley: Shambhala, 1969.

————, *The Myth of Freedom*. The Clear Light Series. Berkeley: Shambhala, 1976.

Trungpa, Chögyam, and Fremantle, Francesca (trs.), *The Tibetan Book of the Dead*. Berkeley, Calif.: Shambhala, 1975.

Tucci, Giuseppe, *The Theory and Practice of the Mandala*. London: Rider and Company, 1969.

von Dürckheim, Karlfried Graf, *Hara, the Vital Centre of Man*. London: George Allen and Unwin, Ltd., 1962.

Warner, Langdon, *The Enduring Art of Japan*. Cambridge, Mass.: Harvard University Press, 1952; New York: Grove Press, 1958.

Warren, Henry Clark, tr., *Buddhism in Translations*. New York: Atheneum, 1963.

Watts, Alan W., *The Way of Zen*. New York: Pantheon Books, Inc., 1957; Vintage, 1974.

Welch, Holmes, *The Buddhist Revival in China*. Cambridge, Mass.: Harvard University Press, 1968.

————, *The Practice of Chinese Buddhism: 1900–1950*. Cambridge, Mass.: Harvard University Press, 1967.

Yokoi, Yūhō, *Zen Master Dōgen: An Introduction with Selected Writings.*
New York and Tokyo: Weatherhill, 1976.
Zimmer, Heinrich (ed. by Joseph Campbell), *The Art of Indian Asia.* 2 vols.
Bollingen Series. New York: Pantheon Books, Inc., 1955.
————, (ed. by Joseph Campbell), *Philosophies of India.* Bollingen Series.
New York: Pantheon Books, Inc., 1951,

# Index

*Grateful acknowledgment is made to the following for permission to reprint previously published material:*

City Lights Books: "Sakyamuni Coming Out from the Mountain," from *Reality Sandwiches* by Allen Ginsberg. Copyright © 1963 by Allen Ginsberg. Reprinted by permission of City Lights Books.

E. P. Dutton & Co. and George Allen & Unwin Ltd.: Excerpts from *The Tantric Mysticism of Tibet* by John Blofeld. Copyright © 1970 by George Allen & Unwin Ltd. Reprinted by permission of E. P. Dutton & Co. and George Allen & Unwin Ltd.

The First Zen Institute of America: Excerpt from *Zen: A Religion* by Ruth Fuller Sasaki. Published by The First Zen Institute of America, New York City, 1958.

Alfred A. Knopf, Inc.: Excerpt from *The Dhammapada: The Sayings of the Buddha*, a new rendering by Thomas Byrom. Copyright © 1976 by Thomas Byrom. Reprinted by permission of Alfred A. Knopf, Inc.

Macmillan Publishing Co., Inc.: Excerpt from *Secrets of the Lotus*, edited by Donald K. Swearer. Copyright © 1971 by Donald K. Swearer. Reprinted with permission of Macmillan Publishing Co., Inc.

Tatiana Nagro: Excerpt from *A New Model of the Universe* by P. D. Ouspensky. Published by Alfred A. Knopf, Inc., New York, 1931.

New Directions Publishing Corp.: Excerpt from *The Asian Journal* of Thomas Merton. Copyright © 1973 by the Trustees of the Merton Legacy Trust. Reprinted by permission of New Directions.

John Weatherhill, Inc.: Excerpt from *Zen Master Dōgen* by Yuhō Yokoi with Daizen Victoria. Reprinted with permission of John Weatherhill, Inc., N.Y.

John Wiley & Sons, Inc., and the Edward W. Hazen Foundation: Excerpt by U Thittila from *The Path of the Buddha*, edited by Kenneth Morgan. Published by John Wiley & Sons, Inc. Reprinted with the permission of the publisher and of the Edward W. Hazen Foundation.

In collecting various illustrations for this book, I received help from, and owe special thanks to, a long list of gracious people and generous institutions. I particularly wish to mention the following (in alphabetical order): Asia Society of New York City; Brandeis University: the Rose Art Museum (Dr. Carl Belz); Breezewood Foundation (Alexander Griswold); Brooklyn Art Museum (Amy Poster, Associate Curator, Department of Oriental Art);

# PERMISSIONS

Mary and Jackson Burke Collection of Japanese Art; Cleveland Art Museum (Sherman E. Lee); Frederick Hamilton; Orrin Hein; Baron Sazo Idemitsu, Tokyo, Japan; Newark Art Museum (Valrae Reynolds, Curator of Oriental Collections); Eleanor Olson, former Curator of Oriental Art, Newark Art Museum; Mr. and Mrs. John D. Rockefeller III Collection of Asian Art (Bertha Saunders); Seattle Art Museum; His Excellency Michiaki Suma, Ambassador of Japan to Canada; Doris Weiner Art Gallery (Isabel Wellisz); and William H. Wolff.

# PERMISSIONS

## ZEN BUDDHISM

## A Note About the Author

Nancy Wilson Ross is a novelist, social historian,
and long-time student of Asian life and thought.
Among her novels are *The Left Hand Is the Dreamer*;
*I, My Ancestor*; and *The Return of Lady Brace*.
She has lived and traveled widely in Asia and has written
for many leading magazines on her extensive travels
and on the customs, art, and religious philosophies of the East.
Her last two non-fiction books, published here and abroad,
have been *The World of Zen* and
*Three Ways of Asian Wisdom: Hinduism, Buddhism, Zen*.

Please remember that this is a library book,
and that it belongs only temporarily to each
person who uses it. Be considerate. Do
not write in this, or any, library book.

WITHDRAWN

294.3 R825b 1981

Ross, Nancy Wilson,
1901-1986.
Buddhism, a way of li'
and thought /
1981  ~199